A2 Psychology

UNIT 4B

Edexcel

Criminological Psychology

Christine Brain

Philip Allan Updates
Market Place
Deddington
Oxfordshire
OX15 0SE

tel: 01869 338652
fax: 01869 337590
e-mail: sales@philipallan.co.uk
www.philipallan.co.uk

ISBN 0 86003 887 4

This Guide has been written specifically to support students preparing for the
Edexcel A2 Psychology Unit 4 examination. The content has been neither
approved nor endorsed by Edexcel and remains the sole responsibility of the
author.

Printed by Raithby, Lawrence & Co. Ltd, Leicester

Contents

Introduction

■ ■ ■

Content Guidance

■ ■ ■

Questions and Answers

Introduction

About this guide

This is a guide to Unit 4B of the Edexcel A2 specification: Criminological Psychology. Before looking at what this guide is all about, here is some good news (in the form of positive reinforcement). You can pass the exam for this unit, and you can do well. How can I draw this conclusion without knowing you? Because you are reading this guide.

Students who take the trouble to read this sort of guide:
- are motivated to do well
- have an idea about where to look for help
- understand what unit they are taking, and with which examination board
- know something about active learning — we can learn better if we engage in tasks, such as using this sort of student guide

So you already have some of the skills and knowledge you need — hence my claim that you can do well. However, this guide:
- is not a textbook — there is no substitute for reading the required material and taking notes
- does not tell you the actual questions on your paper, or give you the answers!

Aims

The aim of this guide is to provide you with a clear understanding of the requirements of Unit 4B of the A2 specification and to advise you on how best to meet these requirements.

This guide will look at:
- the psychology you need to know about
- what you need to be able to do and what skills you need
- how you could go about learning the necessary material
- what is being examined
- what you should expect in the examination for this application
- how you could tackle the different styles of exam question
- the format of the exam, including what questions might look like
- how questions are marked, including examples of answers, with examiner's comments

How to use this guide

A good way to use this guide is to read it through in the order in which it is presented. Alternatively, you can consider each topic in the Content Guidance section, and then turn to the relevant question in the Question and Answer section. Whichever way you use the guide, try some of the questions yourself to test your learning. Hopefully, you will know enough about the marking by this time to try to grade your own answers. If you are working with someone else, mark each other's answers.

The more you work on what is needed, the better. Have other textbooks available too — you will need access to all the relevant information.

Study skills and revision strategies

If you have been studying the Unit 4 material on Criminological Psychology, and have engaged in a reasonable amount of learning up to now, you can make good use of this guide.

This guide can also help if you know very little of the material and have only a short time before the examination. If this describes you, you have a lot of work and long hours of study ahead — but you can do it.

Before reading on, answer the following questions:
- How long is left before the exam?
- Do you have a revision plan?
- Are you sure you want to pass, and hopefully do well? Renewing your motivation can help.
- Are you stressed and in a panic?
- Can you stick to your plan, and trust it?

If you need to, draw up a revision plan now, remind yourself that you do want to succeed, and practise some relaxation techniques.

Revision plan

- Start at least 4 weeks before the exam date (sooner if possible).
- Using times that suit you (6 a.m. might be a great time to study!), draw up a blank timetable for each of the weeks.
- On the timetable, fill in all your urgent commitments (cancel as many plans as you can).
- Divide up what is left, allocating slots to all your subjects as appropriate. Don't forget to build in meal times, breaks and time for sleep.
- Stick to the plan if at all possible, but if you have to, amend it as you go.
- When studying, have frequent, short rests and no distractions.

Time management

Answer the following questions to see how good you are at time management.

(1) Are you usually punctual?
  yes   no

(2) Do you tend to work fast and then correct mistakes?

    yes   no

(3) Do you often put things off?

    yes   no

(4) Do you feel stressed because you never have enough time?

    yes   no

(5) Do you work slowly and carefully, and try to get things right first time?

    yes   no

(6) Do you daydream?

    yes   no

(7) Are you forgetful?

    yes   no

(8) Do you find it hard to get started?

    yes   no

(9) Do you keep your desk tidy?

    yes   no

Score 0 for 'yes' and 1 for 'no' to questions 1, 5 and 9. Score 1 for 'yes' and 0 for 'no' to questions 2, 3, 4, 6, 7 and 8. A score of 3 or below means your time management is quite good; a score of 4 and above means you need to work on it.

Relaxation techniques

Boxes 1, 2 and 3 suggest some ways to relax. Use these as appropriate.

Box 1: Technique 1 — takes about 10 minutes

This technique is useful at the start or end of a longish revision period.

- Lie on the floor and make yourself comfortable.

- Working from toes to head, tense each of your muscles in turn and then relax.

- Having relaxed your body, now relax your thoughts.

- Take yourself in your mind to a place where you feel at peace — this could be a favourite holiday place, or a favourite place on a walk. Closing your eyes will help.

- Have a good look around (mentally!), sit down there and listen to the sounds of the place.

- Stay there and try not to come back yet.

- When you are ready, come back. Slowly start to hear the sounds around you, and lie with your body relaxed for a little while longer.

Box 2: Technique 2 — takes about 5 minutes

This technique is useful as you revise. Work for between 30 minutes and an hour, and then stop to relax as follows:

- Sit comfortably and try to ignore anything going on around you.

- Imagine you are in a barn, sitting on the rafters under the roof, swinging your legs and sitting comfortably. Closing your eyes will help.

- Now, imagine that the barn has open doors at both ends, and there is a river rushing through from one end of the barn to the other. You are sitting swinging your legs, watching the river rush through below you.

- Hear the water rushing through, sit comfortably, and just watch.

- Think of the water as your thoughts rushing away.

- You are not involved, just watching.

- After about 3 minutes or when you are ready, slowly start to hear the sounds around you, and gradually bring your thoughts back into the real world. Look around you for a minute or two and check that you feel better, before getting back to work.

Box 3: Technique 3 — takes about 1 minute

This technique is useful when you are actually in the examination, and can be used if you are too anxious to continue.

- Imagine you are in an exam now.

- Imagine that you are getting anxious.

- Pick up a pen as if to write.

- Hold the pen up in front of you and stare at it.

- Let all your other thoughts go and think about the pen.

- Try to think of nothing else even for a few seconds.

- Get back to work!

Examination structure and skills

Unit 4 consists of five applications of psychology: clinical, criminological, education, work and sport. You must select *two* of these applications to study and you will have to answer questions on both of them in the exam.

There will be three questions for each application which may be divided into separate parts. Although there are three main areas to the specification for each application, there will not be one question for each of these areas. It is not possible to guess what is going to be on the paper — don't try. Prepare answers for all possible questions. If you know the material, read the questions carefully and do what is asked, you will do well.

Assessment objectives

The assessment objectives are listed in the specification. A brief explanation is given below, but check the full list of what you will be assessed on.

Assessment Objective 1: knowledge and understanding (AO1)
- You need to explain your knowledge and understanding of psychological terminology and concepts through appropriate use and application.
- You must demonstrate knowledge and understanding of psychological theories, studies, methods and concepts, as well as psychological principles, perspectives and applications.
- You must communicate clearly and effectively, and present and select material well.

Assessment Objective 2: evaluation and comment (AO2)
You must be able to:
- analyse and evaluate psychological theories and concepts, referring to relevant evidence
- appraise psychological studies and methods

Assessment Objective 3 (AO3)
Assessment Objective 3 is examined in Units 3 and 5, and is not dealt with here.

The Unit 4 exam

Unit 4 is assessed in a 90-minute exam. 72 marks are available — 36 for each application. This means you need to score around 1 mark per minute, with 18 minutes to spare for reading and thinking. In general, you can expect to gain 1 mark for each point that answers the question, or for elaboration of a point. Answers must be communicated 'clearly and effectively' (see AO1 above). Avoid one-word answers and bullet points unless they are asked for. Some Unit 4 papers require you to write an essay at the end of each question, and some do not. You should be prepared to write an essay worth between 12 and 16 marks. Overall, each application has approximately 15 marks for knowledge and understanding (AO1) and 21 marks for evaluation and comment (AO2).

Essay mark scheme
The essays have 2 marks (AO1 marks) available for clarity and communication (use of terms, spelling, ways of expressing points) and 2 marks (AO2 marks) for balance and breadth. In addition, for a 12-mark essay, you need to give four AO1 'knowledge and understanding' points and four AO2 'evaluation and comment' points. For a 14-mark essay, five AO1 points and five AO2 points are required. For a 16-mark essay, six AO1 points and six AO2 points are required.

AO1 and AO2: getting it right
You must be sure to answer the question that is set — you should then cover the AO1 and AO2 skills. The key words in the question (called **injunctions**) guide what you need to write. If you answer the question, you will automatically do what is required.

Table 1 shows some examples of how AO1 injunctions are used and Table 2 shows examples of AO2 injunctions. Note that it is not so much the word itself (e.g. 'describe') that makes it AO1 or AO2, as the whole question. The figures in brackets suggest the mark allocation you might expect for such a question.

Table 1 Examples of AO1 questions/injunctions

Type of question	What is being asked for
Describe a theory... (4)	Say what something is (a theory in this case); this could include an example. Imagine describing the theory to someone who knows little about the subject.
Identify a type of... (1)	Give enough information so that the examiner can understand what is being referred to. For example, if asked to identify a type of attributional bias, the answer might be 'hedonic relevance'.
Name a means of... (1)	Give a name or term. For example, if asked to name a means of controlling aggression, the answer might be 'anger control programme'.
Outline ... (3)	Follow the instruction for describe, but remember that this injunction usually requires less detail, and hence carries fewer marks.
Describe a study... (5)	Try to give the aim of the study, the method, the procedure, the results and the conclusion(s).

Table 2 Examples of AO2 questions/injunctions

Type of question	What is being asked for
Outline a strength of... (2)	You are asked to outline something, so the injunction seems to be AO1 (i.e. knowledge and understanding). However, as what is outlined is a *strength* (in this case), and thus you are being asked to evaluate something, this question would carry AO2 marks. Note, though, that you must still 'outline' (see Table 1).
Evaluate a study... (5)	Give comments, criticisms, good points and so on about a study. Consider strengths and weaknesses of the method, perhaps, or criticisms of ethics involved. Look at alternative findings or consider whether justified conclusions are drawn.
Assess the evidence... (4)	What does the evidence suggest, and how strong is it?

AO1 and AO2: injunctions in essay questions

Essay questions will always involve equal marks for AO1 and AO2. You should demonstrate knowledge and understanding and provide comment and evaluation. Remember spelling and use of terminology (2 AO1 marks for clarity and communication). Remember to address all parts of the question (2 AO2 marks for breadth and balance). Table 3 shows the importance of knowing how AO1 and AO2 marks are split in each examination paper (excluding Unit 3, the coursework element, and Unit 5, which involves some AO3 marks).

Table 3 Approximate mark allocation AO1/AO2

	AO1	AO2	Total
AS Units 1 and 2	42	30	72
A2 Unit 4	28	44	72
A2 Unit 6	36	36	72

Table 3 shows how, for the two AS units, you were assessed more on your knowledge and understanding (58%) than on your ability to comment and evaluate (42%). For Unit 4, you will be assessed more on your ability to comment and evaluate (61%) than on your knowledge and understanding (39%). For Unit 6, your knowledge and understanding and your evaluation and comment skills are assessed equally.

Essentially, then, you have to learn material so you know and understand it, and then plan some criticisms, comments and evaluation points. As a rule of thumb, be sure to learn or plan as many evaluation and comment points as you learn information points.

Conclusions: use of injunctions and AO1/AO2 split

Don't just think of a word in the question as being the whole question. For example, 'describe' is an AO1 command, but 'describe a strength...' is an AO2 injunction. 'Discuss' could signal AO2 marks if you are asked to 'discuss the usefulness of...' Because you are considering how useful something is, you are doing more than showing knowledge about it. The best approach is to *answer the question*. If you study and understand the question, all should be well.

Differences between AS and A2

Although a lot of what is true for AS still applies to A2 — for example, the AO1 and AO2 assessment objectives — the A2 exams require higher-level skills.

At A2, more marks are given for AO2 (evaluation and comment) than for AO1 (knowledge and understanding), except Unit 6 where both skills are assessed equally. This is quite different from what is required at AS. It means you need to comment, evaluate, assess, consider strengths, and so on, more than you need to give information. When you are making notes and preparing answers to exam questions, remember to concentrate on criticisms. Whenever you read an evaluation point, note it down and learn it.

Greater depth is also required in your answers at A2. For example, you could be asked to consider factors affecting jury decision making. The specification does not say that you need studies and evidence, but you do. Remember to refer to the assessment objectives outlined in this introduction. The specification might not ask you specifically to learn studies which show that, for example, zero tolerance has been effective, but you will need to refer to relevant evidence to support your answers (AO2). Psychology is built on evidence from studies, so when revising it is useful to have a list of names of studies and a brief outline of what each is about. Note also that Unit 4 is about applications of psychology, so be ready to apply your knowledge.

Content Guidance

This section provides an overview of what you need to learn for Unit 4B. It includes some AO1 (knowledge and understanding) material for each topic as well as AO2 evaluation points and is divided into the following topics:

The legal aspects of crime

- Eyewitness testimony
- Offender profiling
- Jury decision making
- The just-world hypothesis*
  (* The just-world hypothesis relates more to judgements about guilt than to social influences on crime, so in this guide it appears under legal aspects of crime, while in the specification it comes under the next topic. This does not affect the content covered here or the wording of any questions in the Question and Answer section.)

Social and media influences on criminal behaviour

- The self-fulfilling prophecy
- Media influence on aggressive behaviour

Treating crime

- Controlling aggression
- Zero tolerance and its effectiveness

In the Criminological Psychology section of the specification there are no options as such. However, you can choose different studies as evidence, or different types of attributional bias, for example. If the material here is different from what you have studied, you will need to decide whether to cover this new material or revise what you have learned.

The legal aspects of crime

Eyewitness testimony

> **Tip**
>
> Eyewitness testimony was the key application you studied for the cognitive approach at AS. Recall that information now, as this section builds on what you have already learned.

Eyewitness testimony, in the form of witness statements, is important in tracking down and convicting criminals. However, such statements are not as straight-forward as one might think. This section discusses some of the problems with eye-witness memory, focusing on the areas detailed in the specification. It also focuses on relevant studies because you must be able to describe and evaluate a range of these for this part of the specification. If you have looked at different studies from those given here, then either use the ones you have studied or learn the ones given here as additional examples.

Problems with eyewitness memory

Problems with eyewitness memory might arise due to the following factors.

Length of time of the incident

One problem is estimating the time an incident lasts for. This tends to be over-estimated (Buckhout, 1974).

Confidence levels of witnesses

Witnesses can be more confident than the situation warrants.

Study 1

Clark and Stephenson (1995) asked policemen to recall an incident. Some policemen were alone, some were in pairs and some were in groups of four. All were confident about their recall, with the groups of four being the most accurate, and the most confident — even when wrong.

Attention at encoding

Attention when encoding the information is a problem, as we cannot attend to everything at once, and it is likely that we don't know that we are going to be called upon as a witness of an incident, so we will not attend to what is needed.

Study 2

Buckhout (1980) showed how inaccurate the memory of an eyewitness can be. Television viewers watched a mugging in a New York Street and then saw a line-up of six people, including the mugger. The viewers then telephoned in to identify the mugger with only 14% accuracy.

Bias in storage due to existing schemas

Existing schemas can bias the processing of information, so that it fits with previous experiences.

Study 3

Christianson et al. (1998) asked students, policemen and teachers to watch a video and then tested their recall. Policemen had the best recall — this may be because their schemas were more relevant and more useful.

Problems with accessing memories

Strong associations between objects and events may be more easily recalled from long-term memory than weak associations. Incorrect memories can arise from making the wrong associations.

Consistency of information

The consistency of information is important. We could say that consistent information is more readily available and, therefore, is recalled. An alternative view is that inconsistent information may attract more attention and so be more likely to be encoded. It seems that inconsistency does not help memory if judgements are complex, if there is pre-existing knowledge of the person involved, or if witnesses have had time to think about their impressions of the person.

Leading questions that bias retrieval

Quite a lot of research has been done in this area, including the following studies.

Study 4

Loftus (1975) showed a film of a car accident to approximately 150 students and then asked various questions; some were leading, some were not. For example, she asked how fast a car was going 'when it passed a barn' even though there was no barn, thus leading the witnesses to think about a barn. Of the students with the question about a barn, 17.3% 'recalled' a barn, but only 2.7% of those without that question remembered a barn. This was taken as evidence that we are affected by words in a question — whether leading or misleading.

Study 5

Loftus (1978) showed 195 participants a slide: 95 of them saw a small red Datsun car at a stop sign and 100 saw the car at a give way sign. They saw other slides too. Later in the test, they were asked questions about what they had seen: one questionnaire included a question about a car at a stop sign; another questionnaire had a question about a car at a give way sign. This meant that some participants had questions that were consistent with what they had seen, and some did not. 75% of those with a consistent question (e.g. asking about a stop sign when they had seen a stop sign) had accurate recall, compared with 41% who had an inconsistent question. This suggests that an inconsistent question can bias our recall.

Study 6

Loftus and Palmer (1974) showed participants a film of a car accident and then asked them to estimate the speed of the cars when they 'hit/bumped/collided/

contacted/smashed'. These alternative words were given to different participants. Their estimates of speed were affected just by the change of verb, with 'smashed' producing a higher estimate than 'contacted' (41 mph compared with 32 mph). Participants were later asked about broken glass and those with the word 'smashed' were more likely to recall broken glass (there was none) than those with the word 'hit'. It seems that a word in a question can lead to distortion of recall.

Study 7
Garry et al. (1994) used two brothers in a study. They asked the older brother to tell his 14-year-old younger brother that the younger brother had been lost in a shopping mall when he was a small child. The older brother gave his younger brother correct information as well, and then incorporated the story of being lost in with the rest. When the 14-year-old was asked about the incident 2 weeks later, he recalled being lost and included other information too, which he seemed to have added to the 'memory'.

> **Evaluation**
> + The experiments involved careful controls and the findings have been replicated.
> + The findings of the various studies support one another.
> − In the Garry et al. study, a false memory was implanted, so the ethics of this study should be questioned. This is particularly important as the participant was only 14 years old.
> − Loftus (1997) emphasised that only peripheral information (such as whether a sign was a stop sign or a give way sign) had distorted recall. Central information may be recalled more accurately. For example, when a study was done that involved a red purse being stolen, and the colour was distinctive, 98% of participants recalled the colour of the purse.
> − It may be that a memory itself is accurate, but misleading questions affect retrieval of the memory, although it is hard to test this.
> − Experiments are often not valid (as the above criticisms suggest) as the situations are not natural. In real-life events, the witness would be a participant in a different sense.

Stereotyping
Stereotyping can lead to associations that are not appropriate, because of previous associations. This can lead to bias in eyewitness testimony/memory.

Study 8
Loftus (1979) showed a film with two people (A and B) talking. When later A was seen committing a burglary with a third person (C), participants tended incorrectly to identify B, rather than C, as the burglar's accomplice. It seemed that they had associated A (the burglar) and B and that led them to identify B as the accomplice.

Arousal
The level of arousal can affect recall and in events where we are eyewitnesses we are likely to be highly aroused. Memories are said to be accurate when we are aroused (Hollin, 1989).

Study 9

Loftus et al. (1983) showed some participants a film featuring a fire and showed others a less emotional event. When those who watched the fire were reminded of it, they had *worse* recall. Perhaps the emotion of the event disrupted their recall.

The weapon focus effect

The weapon focus effect might be linked to arousal. Loftus et al. (1987) found that if a weapon was present in a situation, people tended to focus on the weapon — or at least they had less good recall for faces in these situations.

Study 10

Mitchell et al. (1998) suggested that Loftus et al.'s findings were not due to arousal, as even when someone was holding a stick of celery and not a weapon, people focused on that. Perhaps it was that the celery or weapon simply drew people's attention — either was unusual and so was attended to.

Attributions

The reasons we give for actions — both our actions and those of others — are attributions and these can affect eyewitness memory. We take many factors into account when giving reasons for the actions of ourselves and others, including the situation. We give internal reasons, involving disposition or character (dispositional attribution), and external reasons, involving the situation and environment (situational attribution). However, when giving reasons for behaviour we make errors — called **attributional biases**. Some examples are outlined below.

Hedonic relevance

This refers to the personal meaning an event has for us. The more the event has personal meaning, the more likely we are to give dispositional attribution to the actions of others. For example, if people damage our property we are more likely to blame their 'disposition' than to blame the situation, as we are 'attached' to our property and it has hedonic relevance for us. If eyewitnesses have a personal stake in the situation, they are more likely to give detail about the individual, and blame him/her, rather than the situation.

The fundamental attribution error (FAE)

This claims that we tend to blame others dispositionally (saying it is their own fault) whereas when considering ourselves we blame the situation (e.g. we say we could not help it because...). For example, if someone drives into the back of your car you are likely to blame the driver dispositionally, for example by saying he/she is a bad driver. However, if you drive into the back of someone's car you are likely to say that the car had no brake lights — in other words, you blame the situation. A witness is likely to blame another person's disposition, not the situation, and this can bias the account.

The actor–observer effect

This holds that if we are an actor in the situation, we look at the circumstances for reasons for our action(s), yet if we are an observer we look to the actor (another person) as being the cause of something. This is similar to the example given above for the FAE. If we are the actor (we drive into someone's car), then we are likely to blame the situation (situational attribution). If we are an observer, we are likely to blame the actor (for example, when someone else drives into the back of someone else's car) and this is dispositional attribution. This highlights the importance of biases in eyewitness testimony and suggests that there is no such thing as a 'pure' description of events by an eyewitness.

Self-serving bias

This suggests that when it is in our interests to give dispositional reasons for our own actions, we do so. This goes against the fundamental attribution error which claims that we give external situational reasons for our own actions and dispositional internal reasons for the actions of others. For example, when we are successful, we don't want to say it is due to the situation; we want to say it is due to internal reasons and we want to claim credit. This could be about sitting an examination. If we pass, we give dispositional reasons (we worked hard), whereas if we don't pass we give situational reasons (there was noise in the exam room). Witnesses may feel it is in their interests to take credit for some part of the action, and this may lead to their recall being biased.

> **Evaluation**
>
> + Many studies have shown such biases, and tend to support one another — if only to say that attributions do affect witness testimony.
> + Most people's common-sense views match the biases above. For example, it does seem to be the case that if someone is late for work because of traffic, others tend to think that person should have left sooner (dispositional), whereas when we are late ourselves because of traffic, we blame the traffic (situational). This is what the fundamental attribution error claims will occur.
> − Studies tend to be laboratory-based, and these can be criticised as missing any element of emotion or reality, so a person's memory might not be affected as it would be in a real-life situation.

Summary

Factors that affect eyewitness memory

- Length of time between incident and recall
- Confidence of the witness
- Attention at the time
- Biases in recall due to existing schemata
- Problems in accessing information due to common associations
- Consistency of information
- Leading questions
- Stereotyping
- Arousal
- Weapon focus
- Attributional biases

How to improve eyewitness testimony

Shapiro and Penrod (1986)

Shapiro and Penrod (1986) suggested that there is improved recall if the situation where recall takes place is similar to the setting of the incident. This suggests that helping a victim or witness by setting up a similar situation or by helping to recreate the situation mentally will assist recall. It also seems to help both witness and victim memories if evidence is given quite soon after the event.

Cognitive interviews

Police have acted on this research and use cognitive interviews to help the witness to set the scene again and recreate the situation mentally. Police are also made aware of biases such as those outlined above. Cognitive interviews focus on the idea of context reinstatement and giving the witness cues that might trigger memories. It is important that the witness talks about everything, not just what is thought to be important by police interviewers or the witness. Changing perspective can help — the witness can be asked to imagine what another witness may have seen, for example. This can help to avoid too much interpretation on the part of the witness, such as bias that might be caused by reasons the witness attributes to certain events that took place. Changing the order of events can also help — the witness can be asked about what happened before the incident, or could be asked to work backwards through it. These various techniques can help to break down biases. Other important techniques include helping witnesses to relax and letting them do the talking. If the interviewer guides the questions too much, puts pressure on the witness or does not pick up on the focus of the responses, something might easily be missed.

Summary

Improving EWT: cognitive interviews

Improving EWT
- Improved recall occurs if the situation where recall takes place is similar to the setting of the incident
- Helping a victim or witness by setting up a similar situation can aid recall
- Helping to recreate the situation mentally will help recall
- Giving evidence soon after the event can help

Cognitive interviews
- The police are made aware of biases
- Cognitive interviews focus on context reinstatement
- It is important that the witness talks about everything
- Changing perspective can help
- Changing the order of events can help
- These techniques can help to break down biases

The use of hypnosis in victim and witness memory

Forensic hypnosis is used to gather evidence. There is a belief that hypnosis can uncover buried memories and release them into our conscious, so they are recalled. This would be useful for helping victims and witnesses of crime to recall evidence. However, hypnosis has been shown to be ineffective. When participants watched a video of a pickpocket at work and were then later asked about the incident, those who were hypnotised and interviewed in fact recalled less than those who were interviewed but not hypnotised (Sanders and Simmons, 1983). On the other hand, Geiselman and Machlowitz (1987) found that:

- in 21 out of 38 different studies of the use of hypnosis in interviews, the hypnotised participants *did* recall more
- four studies showed that the hypnotised participants gave less information
- 13 studies showed that there was no difference
- in eight studies, those who were hypnotised gave more incorrect information

So even if more information is recalled, it may not be correct. One problem is that the relaxed and suggestible state of those under hypnosis makes them vulnerable to implanted false memories (Orne, 1979). This would be done deliberately, but questioning may lead to false memories, and the individual will have difficulty in distinguishing false memories from true ones. Gibson (1982) said that using hypnosis is like tampering with the evidence, because of the likelihood of the participant picking up cues from the hypnotist and hence recalling false information.

Evaluation

- There is doubt about how helpful hypnosis is as a means of uncovering witness or victim memories. In the suggestible state, a person may well recall more, but the suggestibility itself means that recall is likely to be tampered with or false.
- Laboratory studies are not likely to be reliable. It would be hard to recreate the exact situation and to repeat the study.
- It is hard to control all variables when doing a study involving hypnosis, as there is not just one independent variable that can be isolated. At first sight it might appear that whether someone is hypnotised or not is just such a variable, but in practice there is evidence to suggest that hypnosis is nothing more than a heightened level of suggestibility and relaxation.

Summary

The use of hypnosis in victim and witness memory

Evidence	Evaluation
• Sanders and Simmons (1983) found that participants in a study who were hypnotised recalled less than those who were not hypnotised • Orne (1979) found that those under hypnosis were vulnerable to implanted false memories • Gibson (1982) said using hypnosis is like tampering with the evidence, because of the likelihood of the participant recalling false information	• In the suggestible state of hypnosis, a person may recall more, but the suggestibility itself means that recall is likely to be tampered with or false • Many studies are laboratory-based and so have little validity and are unlikely to be reliable • It is hard to control all variables when a study involves hypnosis

Offender profiling

Offender profiling involves gathering evidence from a crime and crime scene to try to build up information about the likely behaviour and characteristics of the criminal. Evidence comes both from physical aspects of the crime and from behaviour. The scene of the crime is important, as are the characteristics of the victim(s). Those who carry out such profiling in Britain often work in academic settings such as universities; in America they are FBI employees.

Profilers are objective and do not interview suspects or get involved with actual evidence. They use statistics to build up a profile of an individual likely to carry out a particular crime or crimes. This enables the police to focus their investigation; it does not lead directly to the discovery of the actual criminal. An example of profiling is if wounds are inflicted in such a way as to suggest some expertise in medicine. This could help police to narrow down a list of suspects.

Stages in profiling

Investigative phase
During this phase, the aims are to:
- look at linking crimes
- look for possible leads
- give the police ideas about where to look for suspects
- consider issues such as whether the behaviour is likely to lead to more serious crimes

Trial phase
During this phase, further insights are developed. For example:
- the state of mind of the criminal is considered
- the police might be helped to evaluate the evidence
- help might be given on how to carry out interviews
- possible links between crimes are considered

Features of the crime
There is also a consideration of the features of the crime, including:
- the **corpus delicti** (or the body of the crime), which refers to evidence from the scene itself
- the **modus operandi**, which refers to the method of the crime
- **signature behaviours**, which are actions by the criminal that can be used to identify different crimes he or she has carried out, or which can indicate some psychological or emotional information about the criminal

Processes and reasoning in profiling

There are several different types of reasoning and processes used in profiling. Attempts have been made to categorise these types; however, it is not really possible to categorise each method of profiling perfectly. In practice, profilers use more than one type of reasoning, and methods of profiling, that are said to be different, overlap.

Inductive reasoning

Inductive reasoning is when evidence is gathered from the scene and elsewhere, and that evidence is then used to build a picture of what the individual who carried out the crime is likely to be like. If profilers have specific details of a crime to go on, they can use those details to match up with past experience to suggest likely avenues for investigation. However, there is no certainty in their conclusions — they can only be speculations.

Inductive profilers gather data from the scene and from statistics, and then try to match them. This type of profile relies quite heavily on information gathered from past criminals. A database is built from this information and can be used to match the type of crime to a likely type of criminal.

Deductive reasoning

Deductive reasoning is when a conclusion is derived from facts in such a way that the conclusion is bound to be true. There is a logical pattern: if A = B and B = C, then A = C. For example, if all serial murderers are men who are loners and have an interest in gun clubs, and a man who is a loner with an interest in a gun club is one of the suspects, then that suspect is the serial murderer. In practice, you can see that this logic does not work for several reasons:

- It only works if all serial murderers are male loners with an interest in gun clubs, and this is not going to be the case.
- There could be another man who is a loner with an interest in gun clubs (the murderer), so it does not prove it is the suspect in question.
- The above claims that all serial murderers are male loners with an interest in guns; this is not saying that all male loners with an interest in guns are serial murderers.

In practice, deductive reasoning is really inductive too — evidence comes from the external world, and conclusions are only as good as the evidence gathered.

Usually reasoning is inductive and relies on careful analysis of the scene and situation, combined with careful analysis of previous statistics and situations. So if most serial murderers are male, loners and belong to gun clubs (remember this is only an example), then the police may be justified in looking at any such individuals. However, the profile will only suggest avenues of investigation and will not uncover the actual criminal.

A deductive profile is more likely to go from actual evidence, link to other evidence and then draw a conclusion (not using previous statistics and information). One example that has been given is that if there are tyre tracks at the scene, and assuming the criminal probably left the tracks, then it is concluded that the criminal can drive. Unlike an inductive profile where statistics from previous crimes are used, this time the actual crime under investigation is the main focus.

- A deductive profile does not give definite conclusions. In the example given, the tyre tracks may not have been connected with the crime. Even if they were part of the crime, there may have been two people involved, only one of whom was a driver.
- Any profile, whether inductive or deductive, will only ever be an indication of the type of person involved in the crime.
- Evidence will hopefully be gathered over time, so the profile needs to change as the evidence changes. It is an ongoing process.

The US top–down approach

A top–down approach involves drawing conclusions from previous knowledge. Inductive profiling is a top–down approach. It uses statistics from previous crimes to add information to evidence found at the scene of the crime. This type of profiling is often used in the USA, where FBI profilers use information from past crimes to inform searches for criminals. Interviews have been carried out with convicted murderers and experienced investigators and the data are used to produce statistics that match a crime with a type of criminal to give a top–down profile. For example, the FBI is involved in crimes like murder and kidnap, and interviews have allowed it to build a database of information about those who murder and kidnap. From this database, conclusions can be drawn about likely suspects, such as their gender, age, background, whether they are employed and so on. Classifications include organised and disorganised criminals. Of course, there is an investigation looking at specific evidence too, and that evidence is used by the profiler to find a match to a likely type of criminal.

The British bottom–up approach

A bottom–up approach involves using information from external sources, such as what is seen, heard and touched. Conclusions are drawn from what is actually found at the scene. The British approach is a bottom–up approach. It involves working from a crime scene directly and not using statistics from past crimes as much as in the USA. Two examples of the British approach to profiling are outlined below.

Gudjonsson and Haward (1998)

Gudjonsson and Haward (1998) outlined the Torney case, where a policeman was charged with the murder of his wife, son and daughter. The policeman claimed that the son, who was 13 years old, had gone berserk, murdered his mother and sister and then killed himself. A profile suggested that the killing was done calmly and was carried out by someone who knew about guns. It did not seem likely that the 13-year-old had gone berserk. The policeman was convicted of the crimes. This was a bottom–up profile as evidence from the actual scene was the focus.

David Canter (1998)

David Canter (1998) has used geographical consistencies in a crime to identify where a criminal might live. One example of this idea is that criminals often choose locations that are familiar. However, they are not likely to choose a location too close to home. Therefore, they might choose a place that is very like their own. Alternatively, the locations of crimes that might be linked could point to the places the criminal has access to or uses regularly. Evidence is gathered from crime scenes themselves, especially when a criminal has carried out more than one similar crime. Then by mapping the location of the crimes — and other important features — it is possible to draw up a profile of what the criminal is like, where he or she might live, what his/her job might be and so on. This is bottom–up reasoning.

Often, a database of existing crimes is used to predict a profile, i.e. top–down reasoning. The statistics Canter uses, however, involve past crimes that are similar and the information comes from past crimes and criminal patterns rather than from the statements of convicted murderers as in the USA. In Britain, there is more focus on the situation and particular facts about the crime, whereas in the USA there is an emphasis on personality and the type of person who might be the criminal.

Summary

In practice, it is very hard to use only a bottom–up or a top–down approach. Profiling uses both bottom–up and top–down processing, and uses inductive reasoning, so conclusions are never certain. In the USA, a top–down profile is combined with a bottom–up investigation. In Britain, a bottom–up profile is used. Although a database approach is used in Britain, as in the USA, in Britain the data come from other crime scenes and involve a search for patterns using the evidence from particular crimes. In the USA, the database consists of information from convicted murderers and experi-enced investigators which builds a picture of what type of criminal might commit a certain type of crime. Therefore, the two types of database are different.

Evaluation

+ Copson and Holloway (1997) looked at 184 cases where profiling had been used. They found that in 16% of the cases the profiling had helped and in 2.7% of the cases it appeared to have led to identification of the offender.
− Profiles are generalisations and often do not take into account factors about an individual.
− If statistics are used, these are generalisations from crimes, and the people involved in those crimes might be different in many ways from the criminal being sought.
− Information is only from criminals who are known and/or caught, so there is no information about those who have not been caught.
− Innocent people can be questioned because they are the type of person being sought. As profiles are generalisations, this is likely to happen.
− One problem with inductive profiles is that the evidence from past crimes and statistics is based on a small number of such cases, so conclusions are perhaps even more tentative than they seem.
− Any profile is only an idea of what the individual is likely to be like, and is only as good as the evidence gathered and/or the value of relying on similar past cases.
− The interviews with convicted murderers may contain information that has been made up. There is the possibility that those convicted will want to give sensational information to make themselves seem important.

Summary

Offender profiling

The British bottom–up approach	The US top–down approach	Evaluation
• The approach draws conclusions about the criminal from the actual crime scene • Canter has developed a system which takes evidence from the scene (and from other scenes, as profiling is often used when the same person is suspected of many crimes) • Using mapping of various pieces of information, including geographical details, it is possible to draw up a profile of what the offender is like	• The approach uses evidence from past criminal cases to suggest what type of person the offender might be • FBI profilers use a database drawn up from interviews with murderers and investigators • Patterns and statistics are used to predict the type of person who would carry out a particular crime	• In practice, profilers use evidence from the crime itself, past experience and data from a variety of sources. This applies both to the US and to the British approach which are possibly not as different as the headings here imply

Jury decision making

As we have seen, there are problems with eyewitness memory and testimony. Eyewitnesses do not see a crime and then faithfully recall what happened. There are many sources of bias, ranging from how the information is encoded to how it is recalled, including how police interviews take place. These sources of bias are very important to the person charged with the crime, who may well be innocent. Another source of error in the process of moving from an investigation through to charging and convicting someone is the way the jury makes its decision. This is another area where there has been shown to be bias, and that is very important to the person charged with the crime — especially if he or she is innocent.

In Britain, jury members must be over 18 years old, with no convictions and able to understand English. Twelve people are chosen from those called upon. The judge and lawyers can make challenges to prevent someone from being among the final 12 people. This is a process called 'voir dire' and the challenge can either have no reason (peremptory challenge) or can be because it is possible that that person might be biased in some way (challenge for cause).

Case factors that affect jury decision making

There are various factors about a case that can affect a jury's decision making, including pre-trial publicity, the evidence presented and characteristics of the defendant.

Pre-trial publicity

This can bias a jury, so much so that occasionally a case will be abandoned because there has been so much publicity that no unbiased jury is likely to be found. A case can even be dropped part way through if publicity is seen as likely to affect a decision. Fein et al. (1997) used cuttings from the O. J. Simpson case with a mock jury. They found that those who had access to pre-trial publicity were more likely to find the accused guilty (80%). Interestingly, if the pre-trial reporting talked about race, jurors seem to have discounted it as racism and were not so affected by it (45% said 'guilty'), so it seems that the content of the pre-trial publicity is important. Linz and Penrod (1992) carried out a similar study and also found that the decision of a mock jury given access to press cuttings before the trial seemed to be affected by that information.

In England, previous convictions of a defendant are not mentioned in a trial, as it is thought that knowledge of these would affect the jury's decision making. However, sometimes it is hard to avoid the jury having such knowledge, if, for example, the accused has a high profile.

The evidence itself

Jurors strive to make sense of the evidence and build a story using their own schemas. It is likely that each member will interpret at least some parts of the evidence differently as we use our previous experiences and knowledge to interpret information we receive. The defence team tries to present one story, and the prosecution presents a different one. The juror also has his or her own previous experiences on which to draw. The evidence does not give facts that the jury simply has to attend to. These factors are reconstructed and bias can result.

Characteristics of the defendant

Stereotyping is likely to be used to make judgements about the defendant. In our society, it could be claimed that villains are stereotypically unattractive, so the jury may think more kindly of an attractive defendant (Dane and Wrightsman, 1982).

Duncan (1976) shows how stereotyping can affect our judgement of what happens in a situation. Duncan showed White American participants a silent film of one man pushing another man, varying the ethnic background of the men. When a White man was seen to push a Black man, 17% said the behaviour was violent, but when a Black man was seen to push a White man 75% said the behaviour was violent. It was concluded that — at least in that culture — Black men were seen as likely to be more violent, and this sort of stereotyping could affect the decisions of a jury.

Accent has also been shown to affect a jury's decision making. Mahoney and Dixon (1997) found that defendants with 'Brummie' accents were judged as more guilty than those with 'non-Brummie' accents.

Witness factors that affect jury decision making

Eyewitness testimony has been shown to have likely biases, but juries may not be aware of this, so may take eyewitness testimony at face value and base their decisions on such 'facts'. Loftus (1974) set up a mock jury to test this. The jurors had to read a summary of a case. There were three different summaries, and each juror had one of these. In one there was no eyewitness, in one there was an eyewitness whose evidence was accepted unchallenged and in the third one there was an eyewitness who was said to have poor eyesight. The findings showed that where there was no eyewitness 18% found the 'defendant' guilty, yet where there was an unchallenged eyewitness 72% found the defendant guilty. This suggests that a juror is likely to place great emphasis on eyewitness testimony. Even when the eyewitness was said to have poor eyesight, 68% said that the defendant was guilty.

McAllister and Bregman (1976) found that a juror will place less emphasis on eyewitness testimony if it does not actually identify the offender, so the content of the eyewitness testimony is important. Loftus (1980) studied the idea that if a jury was told about the unreliability of eyewitness testimony this would help its judgements. Participants were given descriptions of two cases, in both of which eyewitness testimony was important. One case involved a murder and the other a mild assault. Without being informed about the unreliability of eyewitness testimony 68% found the defendant guilty in the murder case and 47% found the defendant guilty in the assault case. After expert testimony had informed the jury that eyewitness testimony can be biased, 43% said 'guilty' in the murder condition and 35% said 'guilty' in the assault condition. It can be seen from this that the expert testimony did affect the jury's decision. The severity of the crime also seems to affect jury decisions.

Another factor affecting whether eyewitnesses are believed is their confidence. The more confident the witness, the more likely the jury seems to be affected by that evidence. This could help to explain the fairly strong effect of expert testimony, as an expert is likely to be confident or to be seen as confident.

Deliberation factors that affect jury decision making

Once the jury has heard the evidence, and listened to the two stories that the defence and the prosecution have presented, the jurors must go into a separate room and work out a verdict. It is at this point that deliberation between them takes place. At this stage, the decision-making process is affected by various factors, including social pressure and conformity.

Studies have involved putting 12 people together in a room to deliberate about a mock trial and make a decision. Sometimes participants have been those who came to the court as potential jurors but were not chosen. They have watched the trial and become a mock jury for the purposes of study. In Britain, real jurors cannot be questioned, so findings have to come from mock juries. In the USA, however, studies have been carried out on real jurors, although in many states now there is a ban on such questioning, as there is in Britain. One study that was carried out on real jurors found that juries agreed with the judge's summing-up 78% of the time, so their decision was affected by the judge as much as by actual evidence and deliberations.

The deliberation process

Strasser et al. (1982) listed the stages in this deliberation process:

(1) A foreperson is elected. This person is often male and the first person elected onto the jury, as well as being of high economic status. The foreperson often has a strong influence on the verdict. Kerr et al. (1982) found that in San Diego 50% of jurors were female and yet 90% of the forepersons were male — this shows a bias that could be important.

(2) A show of hands establishes what everyone thinks before deliberation begins and is a useful starting point.

(3) The evidence is reviewed before any deliberation starts.

(4) The judge's summing-up is reviewed.

(5) Points about the law are reviewed.

(6) At this stage, deliberations begin.

It seems that what each juror thinks at the start of deliberations affects the final decision. For example, a guilty verdict is more likely if 11 out of 12 think the defendant is guilty from the start. Conversely, if two or more think the defendant is innocent, then a guilty verdict is less likely. This fits with studies looking at conformity, such as those carried out by Asch (1956).

Conformity studies

In conformity studies it is found that if one person is alone in his or her viewpoint in a group, the group's view is likely to dominate, whereas if that one person has an ally, then the group decision is more likely to be changed.

Informational influence is where a juror changes his or her mind because of what others say — that is, they have more or different information available on which to make their decision.

Normative influence is where a juror might change his or her mind simply to conform to the decision of the others, rather than having a real change of mind. In this case, the decision is affected by social pressure, rather than by real evidence or argument. Studies suggest that those who are authoritarian conform more (Crutchfield, 1955) and that females conform more than males (Eagly and Carli, 1981).

Minority influence is where a minority (even as small as one person) persuades the jury to a different opinion. Moscovici has carried out studies that show that people will change to the view of a minority (e.g. Moscovici et al., 1969). Nemeth and Owens (1996) found that if a minority of jurors who disagree with the majority keep up their argument for long enough they can sway the majority in the end. This is particularly true if those in the minority keep up a consistent argument. It seems that having someone disagree makes the others in the group reassess their own views.

Evaluation

+ Many studies have been carried out that show biases that affect how a jury is likely to come to a decision about guilt.

+ Studies often use real crimes and real evidence, so there is some validity, although much of the situation will be unnatural.
– Many studies use mock juries, even if they use summaries of real crimes and real evidence. A mock jury would not have the pressure or emotions of a real jury, so conclusions from such studies are likely to lack validity.

Summary

Jury decision making

Case factors	Witness factors	Deliberation process factors
• Pre-trial publicity • The evidence itself • Characteristics of the defendant	• Biased eyewitness testimony • Expert testimony • Confidence of a witness	• The judge's summing-up • Conformity • Minority influence

The just-world hypothesis

Eyewitnesses to crimes or members of a jury are, as has been outlined, affected by many factors and there are many ways in which our judgements can be biased. There are specific biases to do with the situation, such as whether a weapon is present at the scene of a crime or the race or accent of a defendant. There are also more fundamental beliefs that we hold that could affect how we recall a crime or how we attribute blame in a criminal situation. One fundamental belief is that the world is just, and this can affect our judgements.

The hypothesis

The just-world hypothesis involves an attributional bias and reflects the fundamental attribution error. It is a hypothesis concerning how we make judgements about why crimes take place and who is responsible. Much of the research in this area has been done on crimes involving rape. The just-world hypothesis can be a way of explaining rape — to the detriment of the victim. It has been noted that people seem to blame rape victims themselves, even though it would seem more logical and natural to blame the rapist. This tendency has been studied and is thought to be an example of mis-attribution — placing the blame for an event on the wrong person.

The just-world hypothesis begins with our tendency to see the world as a just and fair place. This is likely to happen, as it makes us feel safe and secure. As part of seeing the world as fair and just, we also assume that people get what they deserve. When this is applied to victims of crimes like rape, the just-world hypothesis predicts that the victim will be to blame for being raped — 'getting what he/she deserves'. The victim is then derogated as an explanation is sought; for example, it might be suggested that the victim should not have been in that particular place, or was wearing provocative clothing.

This is an example of a fundamental attribution error, which helps to keep the judgement that the world is fair, because it proposes that we blame others' disposition (their character) for what happens to them, rather than blaming circumstances. If we blame circumstances, we are saying that these circumstances are not always fair, whereas if we blame the victim we can see the world as fair, and any problems are deserved.

It is also an example of self-serving bias because we can protect ourselves by saying that victims deserve what they get, implying that we would not place ourselves in the same situation. Davidowicz (1975) suggested that many people blame the Jews for their fate as victims of the Holocaust, even though a review of what happened makes it clear that they were not to blame at all. By blaming them, others can remain in their safe belief in a fair and just world. As long as we do nothing to bring problems on ourselves, we will have no problems, as we will get what we deserve.

One study: Lerner and Simmons (1966)

Lerner and Simmons (1966) tested the idea of derogating a victim to keep the idea of a just world. They arranged for an accomplice to be seen to receive 'electric shocks' for giving wrong answers in a learning experiment. Participants simply watched the experiment for a little while; they did not know the shocks were not real, and they did not know that the person receiving the 'shocks' was an accomplice of the researcher.

The participants were then split into two groups. One group was told that it was half way through the study and that they (the participants) could now choose whether the accomplice should (a) be given rewards for the right answers, (b) continue to be 'shocked' or (c) be neither 'shocked' nor rewarded. The other group was told that the 'shocks' would continue. In the group where a decision was possible, all participants opted for the accomplice to be rewarded for right answers or for there to be neither rewards nor 'shocks'. None voted for the 'shocks' to continue.

The final part of the study was to find out how each participant rated the accomplice on a scale of social attractiveness. It was found that those who could make no decision and who saw the accomplice 'shocked' throughout, rated the accomplice as lower in social attractiveness than those who made the decision to stop the 'shocks'.

The conclusion was that those who could stop the 'shocks' did so and, therefore, their idea of fairness was not challenged. However, those who could not stop the 'shocks' would have their idea of a just world challenged. They, therefore, derogated the victim, and found the him/her less socially attractive. There is the implication that the victim is somehow to blame for being 'shocked' and that he or she deserves it. The victim must deserve it as the world is fair and just, so such things would otherwise not happen.

Evaluation

+ The findings help to explain the phenomenon of derogating victims — an idea that seems inexplicable.

+ The participants did seem to believe that shocks were being given, and their different ratings of social attractiveness in the two conditions does seem to represent some idea of derogating the victim.

− The study involved deception of participants, who did not realise that the 'shocks' were not real, and who would have been stressed by watching. Ethical guidelines propose that deception should be avoided, as should stress for participants, so the study can be said to be unethical.

− It was a laboratory study and therefore not natural, so the validity of the findings can be criticised.

− Not all victims are derogated, so there must be more to it. For example, we might only derogate victims when we feel some blame ourselves — perhaps victims we have done harm to, or when we think we might share the same fate.

− Another reason for blaming victims is that we might feel distressed at reading or hearing about an incident. We might be blaming the victims for our own distress.

Summary

The just-world hypothesis		

The hypothesis	Evidence: Lerner and Simmons (1966)	Evaluation
• We believe that the world is fair and just • People get what they deserve • This makes our world stable and predictable • We attribute blame to victims, as they get what they deserve • This helps us to think that bad things won't happen to us • We won't do whatever the victims did to deserve what happened	• A lower level of social attractiveness was indicated when a participant had no power to prevent 'shocks' being given • This showed derogation of a victim to maintain the idea that the world is just	• People do not always blame the victim • Studies tend to be artificial • It does explain attribution that goes against common sense

Social and media influences on criminal behaviour

In this section, the idea that criminal behaviour arises from social influences is examined. One interesting hypothesis deals with labelling and the self-fulfilling prophecy; another important social factor is media influence.

The self-fulfilling prophecy

The self-fulfilling prophecy states that we become what others expect us to become. Our behaviour is received and interpreted by others, and the way they react to what we do and say affects our subsequent actions. For example, if we expect someone to be unfriendly, we behave towards him as if he is unfriendly, perhaps ignoring him. This reaction might well make the individual seem unfriendly, as he is not likely to open up to us if we are ignoring him. Thus the person behaves in an unfriendly way and the prophecy is fulfilled.

Studies

Snyder et al. (1977)

Snyder et al. (1977) found that if we think that a person we are telephoning is attractive, we behave in a friendly way, and the person is helpful. However, if we think the person is unattractive, this might affect how we behave and the person answers in an unfriendly way.

The friendly or unfriendly reaction happens whether the person is actually attractive or not; it is the belief about the person's attractiveness that gives the different reactions on the telephone. When we react to people as if they are attractive, they feel differently and react in a related manner, such as being helpful. This is an example of the self-fulfilling prophecy in practice.

Eden (1990)

Eden (1990) found that when some soldiers selected at random were said to be above average intelligence and others were not, those said to be intelligent did better both in written exams and in weapons tests, even though the claims about intelligence were unfounded. This suggests that there was something about the way they were treated that encouraged them in some way. This is another example of a self-fulfilling prophecy at work.

Criminal behaviour

The same idea can be applied to criminal behaviour. If we expect people to behave against social norms, and react to them in that way, they are indeed likely to fulfil that expectation. The self-fulfilling prophecy leads to labelling. This is when someone is labelled as being a certain sort of person, such as unfriendly, attractive, intelligent or likely to act against social norms.

> **Evaluation**
>
> + The self-fulfilling prophecy can be positive if expectations about behaviour are good (e.g. it predicts that if children are expected to do well, they should do so).
> − It seems that the self-fulfilling prophecy works if people do not know one another, but it does not work well when they know one another as they will have more to go on than simply what they expect in the way of behaviour.

- There are probably other factors involved too, as it does not seem likely that we would immediately accept the reactions of strangers to us, in such a way as to govern our reactions to them — at least not in all cases.
- Other social factors that relate to criminal behaviour can be as strong as or stronger than the self-fulfilling prophecy, which is only part of what affects behaviour. For example, child-rearing style, peer pressure or patterns of interactions within the family can affect whether a person carries out anti-social behaviour. In addition, if members of the family model anti-social behaviour, it is likely to be copied.

Summary

The self-fulfilling prophecy and labelling		
The self-fulfilling prophecy • The reactions of others cause us to respond to them in certain ways • This can cause us to become certain sorts of people and then labelling occurs	**Evidence** • Snyder et al. (1977) showed that the expectations of a person phoning someone affected the behaviour of the one answering — when we react to people as if they are attractive, they feel differently and react in a related manner, such as being helpful • Studies (e.g. Eden, 1990) show that if we behave towards people as if they are intelligent, they are likely to do better, e.g. in exams	**Evaluation** • Evidence from studies seems to show that the way we treat others affects their behaviour • However, it might be that only certain responses have this effect as we may have a strong enough self-image for this not to work • It may also only work if the two people do not know one another

Media influence on aggressive behaviour

Tip

At AS, you studied material that related to the media and how aggression and violence portrayed in the media might lead to aggression and violence in real life. Recall what you know about social learning theory and studies such as those by Bandura.

Defining terms

Aggression can be defined as actions or intentions to harm or gain advantage over someone else. However, these actions or intentions might not involve physical harm. Violence, on the other hand, does involve physical harm. Criminal violence is when the violent actions are against the law. Aggression can lead to violence, so controlling aggression can mean controlling violence, and thus controlling crime. Ways of controlling aggression are considered later in this guide. In this section, both violence and aggression in the media are considered.

Social learning theory

Social learning theory predicts that something that is modelled is likely to be repeated, and it is claimed that models in the media are likely to be imitated. But does aggression and violence shown in the media lead to aggression and violence in real life? Bandura (1973) suggests that we learn through observation, either directly through reinforcement or by observing others. When we learn by watching others, this is vicarious learning. Aggression in the media can lead to vicarious learning or to direct learning if we find rewards in watching such behaviour.

> **Evaluation**
>
> + The strengths of this claim come from the evidence, which is outlined on pp. 34–37, and which is fairly strong.
> − There are other causes of aggression, not related to the media, such as our environment. For example, high temperatures seem to lead to more aggressive behaviour.
> − Freud's ideas would suggest that watching violence can lead to less aggressive behaviour, as it might result in catharsis and a release of aggression.
> − A relationship between aggression in the media and aggressive acts is probably not that straightforward. It is likely that other factors, such as whether aggression is modelled in the family, are important too.
> − Biological factors could cause aggression in people. For example, aggressive tendencies might be genetic and inherited, due to brain damage or caused by deficiencies or excesses in neurotransmitters.

Desensitisation and disinhibition

Two explanations for how the watching of violence on television might lead to violent actions include desensitisation and disinhibition. It is said that we can become desensitised to violence, which means we can get used to it, and initial feelings of shock are unlikely to be maintained, so we come to feel less strongly about it. Disinhibition refers to the possibility that watching actions that are so far outside social norms, such as violent actions, might help to reduce our inhibitions and might lead us to do things we would not otherwise do.

> **Evaluation**
>
> − Studies testing desensitisation have to use mild violence as it would be unethical to expose participants to too much violence to see if they get used to it and therefore carry out more aggressive acts than they usually would. This means that studies lack validity to an extent, as they only focus on mild aggression and violence.

Studies of television violence and aggression and the limitations of methods used

Studies have tested whether watching aggression and violence is likely to lead to aggression and violent behaviour. Films that have been linked to violent crime include *Clockwork Orange*, *Child's Play* and *Natural Born Killers*, but it should not be thought that a direct link has been proved. Some think that there is enough evidence of a link between television violence and real-life aggression for programmes showing violence to be banned (Newson, 1994). However, others think that a more in-depth analysis is needed, as any link between television programmes and real crime is likely to be focused on in newspapers, for example, and, therefore, sensationalised (Cumberbatch, 1994).

Studies looking at violence in the media often choose to look at violence portrayed on television. This is partly because children watch a great deal of television and the effect of children encountering aggression and then possibly becoming aggressive is seen as important. This is because children are developing and more likely to be affected, according to social learning theory.

Some studies involve experiments in which one group of children is shown violent television and another group acts as a control. The researchers see if those who watched the violence show more aggression afterwards. This method is similar to Bandura's initial research where children watched adults carrying out violent acts, although his initial studies did not involve media aggression. Some studies involve carrying out experiments too, but out in the field rather than in a laboratory. Other studies use questionnaires, and others use interviews. Observations are usually involved because the dependent variable (the one that is measured) is usually some form of aggressive behaviour that must be categorised. However, observational methods by themselves are unusual, as the researchers would also need to know what media aggression was involved, as they would need to relate that to any aggressive behaviour.

Parke et al. (1977): a field experiment
Parke et al. (1977) carried out a controlled study using boys in an institution for juvenile offenders. They controlled what television programmes the boys watched. Some watched programmes that included violence, whereas some watched programmes without violence. The researchers wanted to see if watching programmes with violence made those boys do more aggressive acts. Not only did those who watched violence do more violent acts, but also those who watched non-violent programmes were in fact less aggressive than usual. It seemed that watching non-violent television programmes might have a calming effect. This study used careful controls and was a field experiment. A cause-and-effect relationship was thought to have been found.

Evaluation

+ This field experiment had good controls and was carried out carefully. A cause-and-effect relationship was found.

+ There was the additional advantage of the study being in the boys' natural setting, so there was ecological validity. Care was taken to give half the boys non-violent programmes to watch, so there was a control group.
- There might be some ethical considerations, in that the boys' situation was made use of, as they had no real right to withdraw, and those who watched violence on television could have been said to have been made more violent as a result.
- Leyens et al. (1982) did a similar study and noted that the television watching and resultant aggression were singled out factors, whereas in reality there are many influences on behaviour, not just what television programmes are watched. This is a disadvantage of controlled studies.

Singer and Singer (1981): questionnaire

Singer and Singer (1981) issued a questionnaire to parents to find out how much television their children watched. The researchers then observed the children at school to look for a relationship between television viewing and behaviour. It was found that those who watched the most television were the most aggressive. This suggests there is a relationship between television watching and behaviour, as well as suggesting that television watching leads specifically to aggression.

Evaluation

- It would make a difference if the programmes watched involved violence or not, and yet the variable was just how much television was watched. It is likely that the cause of aggressive behaviour at school is more complex than that.
- Although it is possible to time how much television a child watches, it is unlikely that the parents had a very accurate knowledge of this.
- Categorising aggressive behaviour, for example in the playground, is not easy and may not be a reliable or valid measure.

Sheehan (1983): correlational field study

Sheehan (1983) studied children aged 5–10 years old and looked for a correlation between what the children watched on television and whether they showed aggressive behaviour. Peers rated each child according to how likely they were to do acts causing physical harm, and this gave a measure of aggression. Sheehan also asked about the children's aggressive fantasies and gathered information about parents. It was found that there was a correlation between watching violence on television and being aggressive, and that the correlation was stronger for boys than for girls. Other factors, such as child-rearing style (e.g. if the parents rejected the child or if punishment was used) and family income, were also found to be important. Therefore, it is unlikely that there is a straightforward relationship between watching violent television programmes and behaving aggressively.

Evaluation

+ Field studies, such as this one, have validity.
+ Field studies can also have some of the advantages of laboratory experiments,

in that there can be some control of variables, such as the way the dependent variable 'aggression' is measured by peer ratings in this case.

- Sheehan's is a correlational study and so does not uncover a cause-and-effect relationship. Although watching violence on television did seem to relate to violent behaviour, particularly in boys, other factors, such as parental style, were also important.
- In general, field studies do not have the same controls as laboratory experiments, and conclusions must take this into account, so they are less certain.
- Such studies look at short-term effects rather than the long-term effects of watching violence on television when young.

Gerbner et al. (1986)

Gerbner et al. (1986) looked at the content of cartoons and found that there were many violent acts, and also that heroes were likely to be the aggressors. As social learning theory predicts that heroes are likely to be imitated, it can be concluded that the violent behaviour shown on cartoons might well be copied.

Huesmann and Eron (1986): correlational longitudinal study

Huesmann and Eron (1986) carried out a longitudinal study following people's viewing habits over 22 years and found that the more violence people watched on television, the more likely they were to have committed a criminal act by the age of 30.

Evaluation

- + Longitudinal studies are useful as they follow the same participants at different stages in their development. This means that any individual differences are controlled for, unlike in cross-sectional studies.
- This longitudinal study showed a relationship between television viewing and later violence, but factors other than what was watched on television would also have an effect.
- We cannot discount the idea that those who watch violence on television are disposed to violence in the first place. It may not be that watching violence on television leads to aggressive behaviour, but that aggressive tendencies lead to the viewing of violence.
- A problem with longitudinal studies is that so many factors are involved in development that it is hard to pinpoint one (e.g. the effect of watching television violence) and find its effect later.
- Another difficulty is that participants are likely to move or might refuse to take part at some stage. This means that the sample size is likely to be reduced considerably from the start of the study to the end, and bias can occur because of this.

Black and Bevan (1992): questionnaire

Black and Bevan (1992) asked people going to watch a film to complete two questionnaires: one before they watched the film and one afterwards. Those going to watch a film with violence tended to be more aggressive in the first place, and they were even more aggressive after watching the film. This supports the idea that watching violence leads to aggression, but it also supports the idea that those who tend to be more aggressive are more likely to choose to watch violence in the first place.

– It is possible that the questions asked beforehand had an effect on later answers, as participants could have been influenced by questions about violence while watching the film. Perhaps those who watched a violent film focused more on the violence because of the questionnaire, whereas those watching a non-violent film focused more on the lack of violence. This would be a form of demand characteristics.
– With questionnaires there might be social desirability too, and people might answer in the way they think they ought to. There may have been some respondents who realised that it is not the social norm to admit to aggression or violent behaviour, so they may not have mentioned such thoughts.

Meta-analyses

Meta-analyses have been carried out — these involve looking at the conclusions of many studies to see whether an overall conclusion can be found. Wood et al. (1991) did a meta-analysis. They examined 23 studies that looked at television and real-life aggression, and found that, overall, watching violence on television does seem to produce more aggressive behaviour. Comstock and Paik (1991) also did a meta-analysis, this time of more than 1000 studies. They found a clear short-term effect and a correlation between watching television violence and being aggressive later.

+ Meta-analyses are useful as they involve a review of many studies, pooling together the findings to build a body of knowledge. Without these, many findings from different studies would be available, but it would be hard for anyone not working in that field to have an idea of any overall conclusions.
– One problem is that there is comparison of findings from many different types of study which have used a range of methods. This means that all methods tend to be classed as giving equally valid, reliable and generalisable results, which is probably not the case.

Treating crime

This section focuses on ways of treating crime by preventing it and treating criminals to stop them reoffending. It begins by looking at ways of controlling aggression and then considers one initiative — the use of zero tolerance — that might help to prevent crime in the first place. There are, of course, other ways of treating crime and other initiatives that might help to prevent it — the examples considered here are only some of the ways psychology investigates these areas.

Controlling aggression

Tip

You need to study two means of controlling aggression. More than two are given here to help your understanding and to aid your choice.

Modelling

One way of controlling aggression might be to stop modelling it in society. It was suggested on pages 34–37 that violent and aggressive acts in the media are likely to lead to aggression in real life. Social learning theory holds that children learn by observation and imitate what they see. This in turn suggests that if the media show prosocial behaviour, then this might lead to less aggression. Prosocial behaviour involves acts in which people help one another and that model social norms. Thus, one way of controlling aggression is to model less of it, and to model more prosocial behaviour instead.

Cognitive-behavioural therapies (CBT)

Tip

If you have studied clinical psychology as your other application for Unit 4, you will know about cognitive-behavioural therapies, so recall that material here.

The idea behind cognitive therapies is that our thinking patterns guide our behaviour, so if we want to change behaviour, we need to change thinking patterns.

Self-instructional training (SIT)

Self-instructional training (SIT) is one way of helping people to change their thinking patterns. Individuals focus on their thoughts and then change them. For example, negative thoughts can be recognised and changed to positive ones. Helping people to focus on their own thoughts has been shown to improve self-control, and improved self-control can reduce aggression.

Role-taking

Another technique that can be used within cognitive-behavioural therapy is role-taking. To aid understanding of thought processes, someone can take the role of another. For example, young offenders can be helped to take the role of their victims. Chandler (1973) implemented a programme like this and did a follow-up study 18 months later. It was found that the young offenders who had undergone the role-taking programme subsequently had reoffended less than a control group, which consisted of young offenders not on the role-taking programme.

Both role-taking and SIT are cognitive-behavioural therapies, as they focus on studying thought processes and on changing thoughts of offenders so that they are less likely to offend again in the future.

Evaluation

+ Chandler (1973) found that the role-taking programme appeared to work, at least in the short term.
− It is possible that it was the attention the programme gave the young offenders that led to the improvement in behaviour rather than the programme itself. This is the 'Hawthorne effect' which suggests that any participants chosen for a programme will change their behaviour simply as a result of being selected.
− If a programme is thought to work, then a control group that is not put on the programme would, by definition, not be helped. This has ethical implications.
− Cognitive-behavioural therapies may work if the aggressive behaviour is prompted by thought patterns, but may not work if aggression comes from other sources, such as a biochemical imbalance.

Anger control programmes

Anger control programmes focus on cognitive processes too and can help to control aggression. The idea of such programmes is to help individuals to recognise thoughts that precede an aggressive attack and then to help them to change those thoughts. The idea is that thoughts lead to anger, and that the release of tension via anger will relieve pressure. Therefore, individuals learn to become angry, as that anger success-fully relieves their tension.

The three stages of anger control programmes are as follows:
(1) **Cognitive preparation** — where individuals learn to recognise thoughts that precede anger.
(2) **Skills acquisition** — where individuals learn self-control through self-talk. Social skills training or assertiveness training can be useful here. The focus is on behav-iour or control of thoughts that will successfully turn people away from their learnt aggressive responses. Social skills training involves modelling, instructing and role-play. Positive reinforcement is given to encourage appropriate skills. Skills taught vary from non-verbal skills to those required in interactions.
(3) **Application practice** — where situations are set up so that individuals can practise the first two stages. They need to practise becoming aware of their thoughts and overcoming the aggression that follows.

Evaluation

+ McDougall et al. (1987) found that offences were reduced when 18 young offenders who were in prison underwent an anger control programme.
+ Goldstein et al. (1989) found that 15% of those who had undergone an anger control programme and social skills training reoffended, whereas 43% of a control group were arrested again.
+ Goldstein (1986) found in a review of studies of social skills training that skills such as those to do with eye contact and negotiation with others had been learnt.
+ Losel (1995) considered 500 studies of such programmes and found that, overall, there was a 10% drop in reoffending (recidivism), which suggests that at least in some way these programmes work.

- For the programme to work, individuals must be able to focus on their own thoughts and their aggression must stem from anger.
- Even if the programme works in a prison setting, its success may not be transferred once the young offenders return to their own environments.

Behavioural management techniques

Tip

You studied the learning approach and mechanisms of operant conditioning for AS. You may have studied token economy programmes too, as an example of how operant conditioning principles are used to alter human behaviour deliberately. Recall your understanding of operant conditioning principles now.

Token economy programmes

Token economy programmes have been used to help to control aggression. Such programmes are used in institutions and involve operant conditioning principles. The idea is that aggressive behaviour is maladaptive and needs to be changed. The aim is to replace the aggressive behaviour with more appropriate behaviour. That more appropriate behaviour is identified, and might involve, for example, being polite to others or taking part in a team activity calmly. Once the required behaviour is identified, instances of it are rewarded. The individual is given tokens for this approved behaviour and the tokens can be exchanged for something desirable, such as visits or television watching.

The tokens are positive reinforcers. The required behaviour is rewarded and the maladaptive aggressive behaviour is not, so the theory is that the required behaviour will replace the maladapative behaviour. It is possible that as part of the programme the maladaptive behaviour is punished too. Alternatively, negative reinforcement can be used to stop the unwanted behaviour; for example, privileges can be removed if that behaviour is displayed.

Evaluation

- + Studies show that such programmes work in institutions.
- + Training of staff who are to implement the programme is relatively easy and cheap.
- - Staff must consistently reinforce required behaviour, and with different staff this consistency may not be as easy as it seems.
- - Other prisoners also reinforce behaviour, and the behaviour they reinforce is likely to be different from that required by staff.
- - Few long-term studies have been done to see if the effects of the programme last once the individual is released from prison.
- - The learning may not transfer to other situations. The reinforced behaviour is required in prison, but may not be suitable once the person is released. On release, aggressive behaviour may be reinforced once more, by peers or family for example.

   — Control is given to prison staff, so ethical issues must be considered. Social control needs to be carefully monitored, and who is to say what is required or suitable behaviour?

Summary

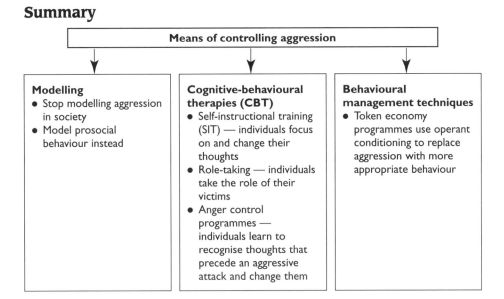

Zero tolerance and its effectiveness

What is zero tolerance?

Zero tolerance when applied to crime means accepting no antisocial behaviour rather than allowing some minor offences to go unpunished. The idea is that if small crimes are allowed, then these can escalate into large crimes, whereas if no crime is allowed to go unpunished, then larger crimes should be reduced. If small crimes are overlooked, then this can lead to a culture of crime, where larger crimes are not seen as so serious.

The idea of zero tolerance is said to have arisen from an article in 1982 entitled 'Broken windows', which was written by Wilson and Kelling. In this article, it was suggested that environment could be a factor leading to crime. Graffiti or some broken windows in an area might suggest that it is not cared for. This might lead to a reduction in inhibitions, a bit like the ideas of disinhibition and desensitisation that were outlined when looking at the effect of the media on aggression. Once an area seems not to be cared for, it is possible that there is seen to be less restriction on criminal acts, and so one broken window can lead to many, and then on to more serious crimes.

Two examples of a zero tolerance policy

New York, 1992

A well-known example of the use of a zero tolerance policy to reduce crime is when New York introduced the idea between 1992 and 1994. The focus was on reduction of street crime in a specific district, and actions targeted included public drinking and drawing graffiti. There was a 25% increase in arrests following the introduction of the policy, which was of course to be expected, as small crimes that would have been overlooked by police led to arrests. Furthermore, there seemed to be a reduction in more serious crime. In 1991 there were 2166 homicides in that district, whereas in 1997 there were 767. Other serious crimes also reduced over the period of the policy.

Edinburgh, 1992

Edinburgh City Council used zero tolerance in an attempt to reduce male violence towards women. This was begun in 1992, and included an advertising campaign and an educational programme. By 2001, a programme called 'Respect' was put into schools with the aim of helping boys and girls to see that violence against women is always unacceptable and should not be tolerated. This educational programme was also supported by an advertising campaign.

The programme was drawn up following a survey that showed that many young people seemed to find violence against women acceptable in some form, and that many said they knew a woman who had been hit by a male partner or who had been sexually abused. The idea was to reduce violent crimes against women by altering the attitudes of young people so that they realised that such crimes should not be tolerated. This is not a zero tolerance policy implemented by police (although they have implemented such policies against domestic violence) so much as instilling a zero tolerance attitude in young people. However, treating crime is still the aim.

> **Tip**
>
> If you use the example of the Edinburgh campaign to reduce male violence towards women, make sure you focus on the way the campaign treats crime by instilling a zero tolerance attitude rather than focusing on the educational impact of the programme. Your answer must focus on the use of zero tolerance in treating crime. Mention how such educational programmes and media campaigns usually have policing policies that support them. (It would not be very useful to change to a zero tolerance attitude if there is no change to a zero tolerance policing policy too.)

How effective is zero tolerance in controlling crime?

To consider the effectiveness of zero tolerance as a means of controlling crime it is necessary to evaluate examples. In general, it is hard to evaluate such policies, as there are many factors that lead to crime and that lead to its reduction, and one policy is not likely to operate independently. An evaluation of the New York (1992) zero tolerance policy demonstrates these difficulties.

Evaluation

+ The evidence of a reduction in serious crimes such as homicide suggests that zero tolerance works.
– However, a lot more police officers (around 7000 more) were put onto the streets to enforce the policy, and this in itself might have led to the reduction in homicides.
– It has been suggested (Bowling, 1999) that the drug market in the area declined at the same time, so this could explain the reduction in more serious crime.
– Pollard (1998) argues that other cities in America also had falling crime rates over the period of the zero tolerance policy in New York, which suggests that other factors account for the fall in crime rather than the policy itself.
– Zero tolerance can mean severe punishments for certain parts of a community. Mentally ill people can be harassed by police as part of the policy of tackling minor crimes. A zero tolerance policy can be aggressive and the police may alienate a community, which can do more harm than good.

Summary

Zero tolerance policy		
Zero tolerance • Zero tolerance means accepting no antisocial behaviour • If no crime is allowed to go unpunished, then larger crimes should be reduced • 'Broken windows' explanation	**Example: New York, 1992** • Focus on street crime • 7000 more police officers on duty • Increase in arrests, but reduction in serious crime such as homicide	**Evaluation of New York, 1992** • The evidence suggests that zero tolerance works • However, there were more police officers, which would itself explain the drop in crime • The drug market in the area declined at the same time • Other cities in America also had falling crime rates • Severe punishments for certain groups, e.g. homeless or mentally ill people • The police may alienate the community

Questions
&
Answers

The questions that follow are presented in three sections, one for each area of the criminological psychology specification:

- The legal aspects of crime
- Social and media influences on criminal behaviour
- Treating crime

Choose one area of the specification and revise the material using this unit guide. Work through the questions for your chosen area, answering them yourself without reading the advice on how to answer the question and without reading the answers given. Then mark your own answers, and read through the advice on what is required. Did you interpret the question successfully? Read through the answers given and note where the marks are awarded. Finally, read through the examiner's comments to see what a full answer should include.

Examiner's comments

All questions and answers are followed by examiner's comments. These are preceded by the icon ℮. They indicate where credit is due and point out areas for improvement, specific problems and common errors such as poor time management, lack of clarity, weak or non-existent development, irrelevance, misinterpretation of the question and mistaken meanings of terms.

The legal aspects of crime

(1) **Discuss studies of eyewitness testimony.** (12 marks, essay)

(2) **Name and outline _two_ types of attributional bias.** (6 marks, AO1)

(3) **How is recall affected by attributional bias? Use at least _two_ types of attributional bias in your answer.** (8 marks, AO2)

(4) **Evaluate evidence concerning the use of hypnosis in memory recall with reference to victim and witness memory.** (6 marks, AO2)

(5) **Compare _two_ types of offender profiling.** (16 marks, essay)

(6) **Outline _two_ influences on jury decision making.** (6 marks, AO1)

(7) **Discuss the effects of social pressure and/or conformity on jury decision making.** (12 marks, essay)

(8) **Describe _one_ study of the effects of characteristics of the defendant on the jury.** (4 marks, AO1)

(9) **Outline what is meant by the just-world hypothesis.** (3 marks, AO1)

(10) **Evaluate the concept of the just world.** (4 marks, AO2)

(1) This is an essay question. 2 marks are for clarity and communication, gained by correct use of terms, good spelling and avoiding note form. 2 marks are for balance and breadth, gained by giving a good balance of AO1 (knowledge and understanding) and AO2 (evaluation and comment), as well as presenting a clear argument. This leaves 4 AO1 marks and 4 AO2 marks. You could choose two studies of eyewitness testimony and look at them in some depth, or you could choose more than two, and look at them more generally.

(2) For this question, you need to name two types of attributional bias from those you have learnt. 1 mark is likely to be for naming the type of bias in each case. Then you must give enough for 2 marks for each short outline, so remember to elaborate on a point or say two things.

(3) For this question, you can either use the same two types of attributional bias you used for question 2 or use different ones. For practice, you should use two different ones. Do not describe them this time. Make sure all your points relate to how the attributional biases affect recall.

(4) This question asks you to focus on evidence, so remember to use evidence from studies in which hypnosis has worked or not worked. Do not discuss hypnosis in general, but focus on how victims and witnesses of crimes have been subjected to hypnosis. Look at the evidence and assess how good it is — this means criticising the studies themselves.

(5) This is an essay question. 2 marks are for clarity and communication, gained by correct use of terms, good spelling and avoiding note form. 2 marks are for balance and breadth, gained by giving a good balance of AO1 (knowledge and understanding) and AO2 (evaluation and comment), as well as presenting a clear argument. This leaves 6 AO1 marks and 6 AO2 marks. You could compare two different types of profiling used in Britain or you could compare a British approach with the American FBI approach. The 6 AO1 marks will be for saying what each approach is. Assume that 3 marks are for describing each approach. The 6 AO2 marks are for saying what the two approaches have in common and where they are different.

(6) 6 marks are available for doing two things, so there are 3 marks for each. 1 mark is likely to be for giving each possible influence on jury decision making, and in each case a further 2 marks are for saying what that influence is.

(7) This is an essay question. 2 marks are for clarity and communication, gained by correct use of terms, good spelling and avoiding note form. 2 marks are for balance and breadth, gained by giving a good balance of AO1 (knowledge and under-standing) and AO2 (evaluation and comment), as well as presenting a clear argument. This leaves 4 AO1 marks and 4 AO2 marks. You can choose to discuss the effects of either social pressure or conformity, or you can look at both. Conformity includes social pressure, but other forms of social pressure could come from other factors, e.g. minority influence. Even responses by jury members to issues such as race and gender can involve social pressure, but you must make the case for this if you use such issues in your answer.

(8) 1 mark is likely to be given for knowing the study itself, and then a further 3 marks are available for describing it. You could give the aim of the study, some brief information about what was done, the results and then conclusions. There are more ways than one for the marks to be achieved, but you need to give more than just one of these factors to get full marks.

(9) There are 3 marks here, so you need to outline the just-world hypothesis quite thoroughly. Explain what the idea of a just world is and say how this is translated into an interpretation of who is to blame in a crime such as rape. You could give an example too.

(10) In this answer, you need to evaluate the just-world hypothesis. You can discuss the idea of a just world and comment on whether this is supported by the evidence. You can also discuss the method(s) used by those who studied the just-world hypothesis — you could criticise these methods and point out that such criticism would undermine the just-world hypothesis.

■ ■ ■

Answers

(1) Studies of eyewitness testimony are important as they point mainly to potential problems. If a defendant is prosecuted and the only evidence rests on eyewitness testimony, studies have shown that there is a serious risk of a miscarriage of justice. ✓ (AO2) Loftus has done many studies in this area and most point to problems with eyewitness and victim memory. For example, Loftus and Palmer (1974) found that if a different verb was used to indicate speed of a car, such as 'hit', 'smashed', 'collided' or 'bumped', then participants gave a different estimate of speed. ✓(AO1) They gave a higher estimate of speed if the word was 'smashed' than if the word was 'collided'. ✓(AO1) The conclusion was that even one word in a question turned it into a leading question, and the word guided judgement, in this case of speed. Another study asked about a 'barn' that was not present in a scene, and yet a number of participants still 'recalled' the barn. ✓(AO1) Leading questions seem to change the memory and this shows that care must be taken when questioning witnesses such as eyewitnesses. ✓(AO1) The studies themselves are not without criticism though. They all tend to be laboratory-based and as such they do not involve any emotion that an eyewitness might be expected to feel. ✓(AO2) Even studies looking at emotional issues tend to be controlled. (For example, those that find that there is a weapon effect, i.e. when a weapon is present, an eyewitness is likely to focus on that rather than on other factors in a scene.) Even if the experiment is a field experiment, controls still tend to mean that the situation is not natural, so validity can be questioned. ✓(AO2)

   📕 This answer is well expressed, uses psychological terms and presents more than one study, so full marks are awarded for clarity and communication and for balance and breadth. The full 4 AO1 marks are easily achieved as the answer considers the study about estimating speed, the one about a 'barn' being present and the study on weapon effect. A mark could have been awarded for the discussion of the weapon effect study, but maximum AO1 marks had already been given. 3 AO2 marks are given. The first is for the introductory comments that studies are important as they show we must question eyewitness testimony so that defendants have a fair trial. A second AO2 mark is given for the comment that laboratory studies exclude emotions that would normally be present. The third AO2 mark is given for the comment about controls making studies unnatural. The final AO2 mark could have been earned by adding that Loftus herself points out that it tends to be peripheral information that misleads people, rather than central evidence, and studies often focus on peripheral information (such as the 'barn'). This answer scores **11 out of 12 marks**.

(2) One type of attributional bias is the fundamental attribution error (FAE). ✓ This refers to the tendency we have to attribute dispositional blame to others, which means we look at other people's characters and disposition and blame them for their actions. ✓ The 'error' part is that we don't do this when looking at reasons for our own actions. For our own actions we blame the situation and not our character. Even for the same event, if someone else does it we blame his/her character, while if we do it we blame the situation. ✓ Another type of attributional bias is hedonic relevance. ✓

   📕 This answer gets all 3 AO1 marks for one source of attributional bias, the FAE. However, only 1 mark is given for the other type of bias, hedonic relevance, as no more is said about it. The other 2 marks could have been gained by saying what hedonic relevance is and giving an example.

(3) The actor–observer effect is a type of attributional bias that has been shown to affect recall. If we are the actor in a situation, then we give different reasons for actions than if we are just an observer. When we give reasons for actions we affect our own recall. For example, if we are just an observer, then the actor–observer effect predicts that we blame an individual for his or her own actions, whereas if we are the actor, we blame the situation or circumstances for our actions. ✓✓ An eyewitness to a crime may be only an observer, so any comments made about those carrying out the crime are likely to be focused on them as people, as the observer is looking at the way the individuals are acting. However, if the eye-witness is an actor in the situation, for example the cashier when money is being de-manded, he might see things differently, focusing on the situation more, and may then recall different things from the eyewitness who is an observer. ✓✓ Another type of attributional bias that might affect recall is self-serving bias. Using the same example of a crime where money is being demanded from a cashier, the observing eyewitness may recall differently from the 'acting' eyewitness. This time the cashier's recall may be affected by self-serving bias as he may feel that he should have been more professional, so in order to seem good at his job he may have altered his recall of events. ✓✓ He may recall the person demanding money as being more menacing than they actually were, for example, so that he can justify his own reaction of handing the money over quickly. ✓✓

> 📖 This is a good answer which focuses on the question well. Two types of attributional bias are given and in both cases the focus is on how recall of eyewitnesses can be affected by such biases. Double ticks are given because each statement that shows how recall is affected is credited, and in each case the statement is set up with a clear description of the type of bias itself. The description of the bias does not in itself gain a mark, as that would not be answering the question; however, the way recall is affected is made clear by the description, so the whole is worth 2 marks in each case. Examples are used successfully to illustrate the points made and are focused on the area of criminological psychology, which is appropriate. Full marks are given.

(4) Evidence suggests that the use of hypnosis to aid victim and eyewitness recall is, in general, not helpful. The hypnosis itself was shown by Sanders and Simmons (1983) not to be useful and they found that participants who were hypnotised after watching a video of a crime recalled less than those who were not hypnotised. However, this was an artificial study. It could be that with a real crime there are sufficient differences to do with emotions of the situation that recall is different, and that hypnosis would have an effect. It is not at all clear what happens during hypnosis and perhaps being part of an artificial study meant that findings were not valid. ✓✓ Geiselman and Machlowitz (1987) tried to find out if hypnosis works and found varied results when they looked at 38 studies. Some showed hypnosis was successful, but more found that it was not. Although some studies found that participants recalled more when hypnotised, unfortunately they also recalled more incorrect information. Again this meta-analysis can be criticised. These 38 studies used different methods and so it is hard to compare results. ✓ Most studies are laboratory-based, using unnatural situations, so findings may not be valid. On the other hand, using false situations is more ethical. If real victims or eyewitnesses were used, then this would not be ethical partly because of the stress on the individual and partly because real evidence would be being considered and could be tampered with. ✓✓ One problem with evidence about whether hypnosis is useful to get at victim and eyewitness memories is that studies using hypnosis also incorporate other factors that go with the hypnosis, such as the relaxed state and the state of suggestibility. It could be that even in studies where hypnosis seems to work, it is the relaxed state and the state of being suggestible that leads to greater recall and not hypnosis as such. ✓(✓) In experiments, it is quite easy to tell if the hypnosis is giving accurate recall as the situation was set up in the first place. In real life, on the other hand, it would not be so easy as it would often only be the victim or the eyewitness who could say what really happened. (✓)

> 🖉 This answer scores full marks and in fact contains enough for 8 marks. All 8 marks are indicated to show how they could have been gained, although only 6 are credited. The first double marks are given for outlining one example of evidence and then criticising its validity. Another mark is given for the criticism of meta-analyses. 2 marks are given for the points about ethics: first, that using real-life victims and eyewitnesses would be stressful for them; second, the point that their evidence is too important to be tampered with as part of a study. The final mark is given for pointing out that one problem is that we cannot tell if it is the hypnosis that aids recall (if it does) or the relaxed state that goes with it. This is worth 2 marks, but full marks have already been gained. The final point could also have gained a mark.

(5) Types of offender profiling include bottom–up and top–down methods. Top–down methods involve using a database of previous information gained from criminals who have been sentenced and from experienced law enforcement agents. ✓(AO1) The FBI in America uses this method. ✓(AO1) The investigators apply previous understanding of certain crimes (predominantly murder) to a current crime to try to work out a likely profile of the offender. ✓(AO1)

Bottom–up methods, however, start from the current crime itself and work up through the evidence to produce a likely profile. ✓(AO1) Bottom–up profiling takes all available evidence and suggests avenues for investigation. ✓(AO1) These avenues are more likely to be specific, such as the type of job the offender is likely to have, whereas the USA profile is likely to be more general, such as the offender's likely gender, race and age. ✓✓(AO2). In practice, both approaches use previous experience and evidence from the crime itself, so they may not be as different as is supposed. ✓(AO2)

> 🖉 This essay achieves full balance/breadth and clarity/communication marks. 3 AO1 marks are given for the description of the top–down method. 2 AO1 marks are given for a description of the bottom–up approach. 2 AO2 marks are given for saying that the bottom–up profile is likely to lead to more specific factors than the

USA profile — 1 mark for making the point, 1 mark for the useful examples. Another AO2 mark is given for showing how the approaches might not be that different — a further mark could have been gained here by giving an example or elaborating upon this point. The final 2 AO2 marks could have been gained by showing that, in practice, there are different ways of going about the bottom–up approach, as statistics from previous crimes can often be used. For example, profiling is often more useful when crimes are linked than for single crimes — when they are linked, information from the earlier crimes informs the later profile. Although this is not the same as using statements from criminals and experts, it is still using previous statistics, so bottom–up and top–down profiles are similar in this respect. If there are different ways of going about each type of profile, then comparing them as if they are specific types of profile may not be appropriate. This answer scores 12 out of 16 marks.

(6) One influence on jury decision making is pre-trial publicity. ✓ If the jurors have read about the crime and the defendant before the trial starts, then they are likely to be influenced by what has been said. This is recognised and so if there is too much pre-trial publicity, a trial may be stopped or abandoned. ✓ Another influence is the evidence itself. It has been shown that we reconstruct our recall of a situation based on our own experiences and understanding, so in a trial, members of the jury will be making their own story out of events. ✓✓ This can be biased by their past experiences, which can affect their decision making.

> This answer scores 4 out of 6 marks. Two influences are named, for 1 mark each. 1 mark is given for saying that pre-trial publicity can mean a trial is stopped, but more is needed for the other mark. An example could be given, where a trial has actually been stopped or abandoned. Alternatively, evidence from a study such as Linz and Penrod (1992), which supports the claim that pre-trial publicity is important, could be outlined. 1 mark is given for explaining a problem with the evidence itself and how reconstruction could take place and might bias decision making. Again, more is needed for the other mark. More evidence could be given, such as Bartlett's (1932) original findings, or the point could be expanded by referring to the 'stories' of the defence and the prosecution as well as the juror's own 'story'. These can become confused and can influence the final decision.

(7) Conformity is a form of social pressure. A jury can be said to be affected by social pressures from the start of the experience through to making judgement on the verdict, in so much as we are all affected by social norms when fulfilling any social role, including being a juror. One stage of jury decision making that is particularly affected by social pressure, such as the pressure to conform, is during the deliberation process. ✓(AO1) This is when the 12 members of the jury are separated and left to come to a decision — which should be a unanimous one. Early in this deliberation process, they have a show of hands to see what each individual thinks. It might be hard for conformity to affect this show of hands, as the individuals won't have the opportunity to see what the others think. ✓(AO2) However, they have had the judge's summing up, and if they are nervous about what they should do they may well conform to this expert opinion from the start. Indeed, it was found that 78% of jury decisions agree with the judge's summing up, which seems to reinforce the idea that this kind of social pressure occurs. ✓(AO2) After the show of hands, the jurors discuss the evidence. Asch (1956) showed that if a group holds one opinion, and only one person disagrees, it is likely that that person will come around to the group's opinion. It seems that if out of 12 jurors only one holds a different view, that person is likely to be persuaded by the rest. ✓(AO1) If, however, more than one disagrees, then these two (or more) can sway the others. So if two of the 12 jurors think the person is innocent, even though ten think the person is guilty, these two can succeed in getting their verdict accepted by the others. ✓(AO1)

One type of conformity is informational influence. If this occurs within a jury, it means that a single person who disagrees with the others conforms because he or she is persuaded by argument that his or her opinion is wrong. It is information that persuades them. ✓(AO1) Another type of conformity is normative influence, which means that the single person conforms just to belong to the group. This type of conformity would be down to social pressure, and would have nothing to do with the evidence or the arguments, which is worrying for the defendant. This is because the one person might think the defendant is innocent but might be persuaded to say he or she is guilty. If the defendant is innocent, he or she will be convicted at least in part because of social norms rather than because of the evidence. ✓(AO2) Moscovici carried out studies that showed that in fact there can be minority influence and even one person can persuade the rest of the group to change their mind. This contradicts Asch's findings that one person will not stand out on his/her own, and that conformity will occur. ✓(AO2) In this case, there must be other factors at work besides conformity, such as the type of person who is dissenting perhaps.

🖉 There is more than enough here for full marks. This essay is well written and uses appropriate terminology, so 2 clarity and communication marks are given. It focuses well on the question and is balanced, so 2 balance and breadth marks are also given. The first sentences are not very well focused and make some general points about social pressure. However, 1 AO1 mark is given for that introductory material together with the point that the main area where conformity may occur is in the deliberation process. 3 further AO1 marks are given for the material on Asch and its expansion and for the material on informational influence. If there were more AO1 marks available, more could be given for the material on normative influence. 2 AO2 marks are given for the point about the show of hands not being affected, together with the material on how the expert opinion of the judge could be seen as social pressure. 1 AO2 mark is then given for commenting that normative influence is more social pressure as the person is not conforming so much as simply stating that he/she agrees. A final AO2 mark is given for saying that the idea of minority influence contradicts what Asch says about conformity. A further AO2 mark could have been given for the expansion on this, saying that perhaps individual differences are important in deciding whether a single juror can sway the other eleven, but maximum AO2 marks had already been awarded.

(8) One study that looks at the characteristics of the defendant and can be applied to the effect these may have on a jury is that done by Duncan (1976). ✓ The aim was to see whether the race of a person affects participants' judgements about how violent the one who was pushing the other was. ✓ The independent variable was whether the actor in a scene was Black or White. Participants were shown a silent film in which one man pushed another man. ✓ If a Black man pushed a White man, 75% of participants said that the behaviour was violent, whereas if a White man pushed a Black man, only 17% said the behaviour was violent. ✓ It was concluded that some sort of stereotyping had occurred and that people (the participants were American and White) judged Black men as more aggressive than White men. The idea is that race as a characteristic of a defendant might already trigger some beliefs in the minds of the jurors, perhaps based on stereotyping, and these beliefs might affect the jury's decision.

> *e* This answer has enough detail for more than the maximum 4 marks. 1 mark is given for the study, 1 mark for the aim and 1 mark for the procedure. A final mark is given for the results; the conclusion could have gained more marks.

(9) The just-world hypothesis rests on the belief we have that the world is just and fair. ✓

> *e* This is a good start, which earns 1 mark, but more is needed for the other 2 marks. It is necessary to say that if this belief is threatened in any way, we might deny what happened to threaten the belief rather than altering the belief. For example, if someone is raped, this threatens our belief in a just and fair world. However, if we can somehow blame the victim of the rape, then it becomes the victim's own fault and so the world is fair and just after all.

(10) The just-world hypothesis helps to explain the seemingly inexplicable tendency that there is to blame a rape victim. People have been known to say that a female victim of rape was asking for trouble by dressing provocatively, and to use such statements to blame the victim. ✓ This seems a strange reaction to such a violent crime, but it does serve to make the world seem more predictable and safer. If we live in a world where people get what they deserve and deserve what they get, then there must be some logical reason for this person having been raped. ✓ However, it is not the case that we always blame a victim in this way, and not everyone would blame the victim in this case. Studies have shown that we are more likely to blame what seems to be a 'slightly innocent' victim, as such a victim would threaten our belief in a just world even more. A 'really innocent' victim does not tend to be blamed at all. One problem with the just-world explanation is that studies that have uncovered such a belief are largely experiments in which situations are recreated. ✓ One such study is that done by Lerner and Simmons who found that participants justified shocks being given to a 'learner' by saying that those people were less socially attractive. Although we could link the findings to the just-world hypothesis and to how we judge victims of rape, what was tested in this study is quite a long way away from real-life crime and so the findings might not be valid. ✓

ℓ This answer gets the full 4 marks for making two points. The first point is that this explanation matches up with what we know happens in real life, and is appealing as it explains what seems inexplicable. The second point is that studies tend to be artificial, so findings might not be valid. In between these two points the answer looks at how some victims are blamed more than others. This is useful material for explaining the hypothesis but not for evaluating it, as it is part of the findings of studies rather than being a criticism or comment of the hypothesis itself. The answer moves back to comment and evaluation when looking at the studies, which gains more marks.

Social and media influences on criminal behaviour

(1) Describe *one* study that investigated the effects of media on aggressive
behaviour. (6 marks, AO1)

(2) Evaluate the study you described in question 1. (5 marks, AO2)

(3) What is meant by the term 'self-fulfilling prophecy'? (3 marks, AO1)

(4) Discuss the self-fulfilling prophecy with regard to antisocial behaviour. (12 marks, essay)

(5) Discuss *two* limitations of research methods used when studying the
effects of the media on aggressive behaviour. (12 marks, essay)

(6) Compare *two* studies into the effects of media on aggressive
behaviour. (16 marks, essay)

(1) 1 mark may be for knowing a relevant study, which leaves 5 marks for description.
Give the aim of the study, some details of the procedure, results and then
conclusions. Remember that often no more than 2 marks are given for each of
these factors, so don't just give one of them (for example, what was done).

(2) To evaluate a study, you might criticise the method used, including looking at ethical
issues. You could give alternative findings from other studies, or you could evaluate
the theory underpinning the study.

(3) There are 3 marks here for saying what a self-fulfilling prophecy is, so make sure
you write enough. If you give an example, make sure it relates to crime in some
way. An example can be useful, but is likely to get only 1 mark.

(4) This is an essay question. 2 marks are for clarity and communication, gained by
correct use of terms, good spelling and avoiding note form. 2 marks are for balance
and breadth, gained by giving a good balance of AO1 (knowledge and understanding) and AO2 (evaluation and comment), as well as presenting a clear
argument. This leaves 4 AO1 marks and 4 AO2 marks. Describe the self-fulfilling
prophecy for the AO1 marks. For the AO2 marks, consider how far this idea
explains criminal behaviour. Perhaps it explains some elements but not others. You
could also criticise methods used in the studies that suggest there is such a
prophecy.

(5) This is an essay question. 2 marks are for clarity and communication, gained by
correct use of terms, good spelling and avoiding note form. 2 marks are for
balance and breadth, gained by giving a good balance of AO1 (knowledge and
understanding) and AO2 (evaluation and comment), as well as presenting a clear
argument. This leaves 4 AO1 marks and 4 AO2 marks for discussion of two
limitations of research. Assume there are 2 AO1 and 2 AO2 marks for each
limitation. Remember to focus specifically on problems with methods.

(6) This is an essay question. 2 marks are for clarity and communication, gained by correct use of terms, good spelling and avoiding note form. 2 marks are for balance and breadth, gained by giving a good balance of AO1 (knowledge and under-standing) and AO2 (evaluation and comment), as well as presenting a clear argument. This leaves 6 AO1 marks and 6 AO2 marks. The AO1 marks are for describing the two studies, so assume there are 3 marks available for each. The 6 AO2 marks are for comparing the two studies. Consider whether both studies say that media affects aggression, or whether they have different findings. Look at the methods used by each, as perhaps these are different, and one gives stronger conclusions than the other. Consider, too, when the studies were carried out, as perhaps they were done at different times.

■ ■ ■

Answers

(1) Parke et al. (1977) ✓ conducted a field experiment that showed that watching violence on television did seem to lead to more aggressive behaviour. The partic-ipants were boys in an institution. ✓ They were split into two groups. One group watched television programmes of which some included violence and the other group watched television programmes with no violence. ✓ Then the boys were observed to see how aggressively they behaved. ✓ Those who had watched violent acts were more aggressive and those who had not were less aggressive. ✓ This suggests that boys model their behaviour on what they see, including television programmes. ✓

e This answer just about earns the 6 marks available. 1 mark is for the study itself. Another mark is given for the overall information — that it was a field experiment carried out on boys in an institution. One problem is that many studies into this area had two groups of participants where one watched television violence and one did not. The mention of 'institution' identifies a specific study. A general description of one group watching violence and one not would not be specific enough. It is clear here that this specific study is understood, so a mark is given for general information in this case. 1 mark is also given for saying that the boys were observed and their aggression noted — even though that too could apply to any study. If this was awarded without the specific detail given earlier, it would be hard to credit it as being about a specific study. A final mark is given for the conclusion that boys seem to model their behaviour on what they see on television. A little more information about the actual study would improve the answer — perhaps saying that it is part of a set of studies that were carried out, and that the others reinforced the conclusions of this study.

(2) Parke et al. (1977) did a field experiment and this method has both advantages and disadvantages. One advantage is that in a field study the behaviour tends to be more natural. The boys lived in the institution where the study took place and were used to watching television there, so to an extent conclusions are valid. ✓✓ However, it was an experiment, so the IV was manipulated. This means there is an element of artificiality in the set-up of the study. The boys would have known that each of the two groups was watching different programmes and would probably have discussed this. ✓ There may have been an element of demand characteristics as the boys may have realised the aim of the study. ✓

> 📝 This answer is awarded 4 of the 5 marks available. The focus is on evaluation so the question is answered appropriately. A double mark is given for the comment about behaviour being more natural in a field study and the elaboration of that comment. Then 2 marks are given for ideas of how the manipulation of the IV might have led to a lack of validity in the conclusions. The final mark could have been gained by considering the ethics of the study. The boys were already in an institution and may have been forced to take part in the study, which goes against the guideline requiring their informed consent (and they may not have had the right to withdraw).

(3) The self-fulfilling prophecy is when people believe that the world is a just and fair place and that people get what they deserve.

> 📝 This answer is not correct as what is written clearly applies to the just-world hypothesis and not to the self-fulfilling prophecy. No marks are awarded. The 3 marks could have been gained by outlining the self-fulfilling prophecy and perhaps giving an example to make it clear, as it is not easy to explain.

(4) The self-fulfilling prophecy is often used with reference to education but can be applied to antisocial behaviour. The idea is that people react to the expectation of others. If people have an expectation about someone, that person is likely to act in accordance with that expectation. ✓ (AO1) It follows that if someone is thought of as likely to carry out criminal behaviour, he or she may respond by doing just that. It could be that someone is part of a group of youths who act in an aggressive manner. On meeting people who know this, the individual could be treated as if he/she were aggressive (perhaps by someone being aggressive to them in turn) and this could lead the individual into the expected aggressive behaviour. ✓✓ (AO1) Snyder et al. (1977) found that if we think someone on the other end of a telephone is attractive, we behave towards the person in a way that leads him/her to react in a pleasant manner, whereas if we think the person is unattractive, we behave in such a way as to get unhelpful behaviour. This shows the self-fulfilling prophecy in action. ✓ (AO1) The prophecy leads to labelling, and labelling is a theory often applied as an explanation of criminal behaviour.

The self-fulfilling prophecy is unlikely to be a complete explanation of antisocial behaviour. The initial expectation is likely to come from somewhere. It could be that a family is known to behave antisocially so any member of that family might be expected to act in a similar way, and this can lead to a self-fulfilling prophecy. ✓ (AO2) However, it could be that the family member acts in an antisocial way through modelling on other family members, and this can be explained by the social learning theory rather than by a self-fulfilling prophecy. ✓ (AO2) It is useful to know about the prophecy, as then steps can be taken by those in authority, such as teachers in schools and members of the police, not to show expectations about the behaviour of others — at least not negative ones. ✓ (AO2) If people know each other well, the self-fulfilling prophecy is not likely to work as there would be few unfounded expectations. Expectations about behaviour would be based on previous experience instead. ✓ (AO2)

> *e* This essay focuses on describing the prophecy in relation to antisocial behaviour and then commenting on its usefulness, so it is awarded 2 balance and breadth marks. 2 clarity and communication marks are also given for use of appropriate terms and good communication. Maximum AO1 and AO2 marks are awarded. The self-fulfilling prophecy is clearly outlined with relevant examples and one study. Comments then include one about the usefulness of knowing about the prophecy, and ideas about what else could cause antisocial behaviour, as well as one about instances when the self-fulfilling prophecy is unlikely to be in action.

(5) Many different research methods are used to study the effects of media on aggressive behaviour, but the main procedure, focusing on television, is to show violence on television to one group and non-violent television programmes to another group, and then to see how much aggression there is in their behaviour. Participants tend to be children. Limitations of methods include the fact that many studies are unnatural experiments so the findings lack validity, and that many show a correlation between television violence and aggression rather than a direct relationship. ✓✓ (AO1) Experiments have strict controls, and where there are such controls, situations are unnatural. The setting is often controlled, because the main group and the control group must be carefully separated, and the independent variable is controlled, because the main group and the control group must have everything the same except, in this case, whether they see violence on television or not. ✓(AO1) For example, the non-violent television programmes ought to be the same in every way except for the violent acts — although this is hard to establish. These controls — of the setting and the IV — tend to mean a lack of validity and findings might not represent real life. ✓(AO2)

Correlations can be carried out, such as finding out about television watching habits (real-life ones this time) and looking at the amount of aggression shown (such as when playing in a school playground) and then seeing if the more violent television programmes watched means more aggression is shown. ✓(AO1) However, the problem is that there may be other factors responsible for the aggression, i.e. not just the watching of television. For example, a family might watch a lot of violent television programmes and aggression might be modelled. A child might be more aggressive through modelling on the family rather than from watching the television. ✓✓(AO2)

> *e* This essay achieves full balance/breadth and clarity/communication marks as it is structured and ideas are communicated well. 4 AO1 marks are given. 2 AO1

marks are for the two limitations (lack of validity of experiments and lack of certainty of correlations). The other 2 AO1 marks are given later for description of these two limitations. AO2 marks are given for the idea that other explanations are possible with correlations, such as behaviour that is modelled in the family and also for the point about lack of validity with experiments. It is not easy to separate AO1 and AO2 marks for this essay. AO1 marks are given for the description of the method leading up to the limitation and AO2 marks for spelling out the limitation itself. If the comment about it being hard to establish the similarity of the television programmes watched (except for the violent content) was expanded upon, the final AO2 mark could have been awarded. Overall, this essay scores **11 out of 12 marks.**

(6) Two studies that look at how the media can lead to aggressive behaviour are Sheehan (1983) and Black and Bevan (1992). ✓✓(AO1) Sheehan was looking for a relationship between how much a child watched violence on television and how far the child's behaviour was aggressive. ✓(AO1) The children were rated for aggression by their peers. A survey of their parents gave their television viewing habits and other information. Then the two sets of data were put together to see if children who were more likely to harm their peers also watched a lot of violent television. ✓(AO1) This relationship was found and was stronger for boys. It was also found that there were family factors which could have led to the aggressive behaviour as well as the watching of television violence.

Black and Bevan also used a questionnaire but, unlike Sheehan, they did not actually look at aggressive behaviour itself. ✓(AO2) They used adult participants, whereas Sheehan used children aged 5–10 years. ✓(AO2) Black and Bevan asked participants to complete a questionnaire before going to watch a film — a film that the participants had chosen to watch without being part of a study. The participants then watched the film. ✓(AO1) Then the researchers asked them to complete another questionnaire. The questionnaires gave a measure of aggression for each person. It was found that those who were more aggressive chose to watch more violent films, and those who had watched a more violent film were even more aggressive after watching the film. ✓(AO1) It seems that choice of what to watch is affected by how aggressive someone is, as well as the film affecting their behaviour afterwards. Sheehan focused on what parents said about the children's viewing habits, and it is assumed that the children had the choice of what to watch, just as the adults did in the other study, but that may not be the case. ✓(AO2)

The two studies both conclude that watching violence in the media leads to aggressive behaviour, ✓(AO2) but there are differences in the age groups studied, methods used, questions asked and conclusions reached. ✓(AO2) Of course, the adults in the Black and Bevan study may have, as children, been in families that watched a lot of violence on television, and the findings of that study may have been a consequence of what was found in the Sheehan study. ✓(AO2) *e* This essay focuses well on the question and uses good terminology, so achieves full balance/breadth and clarity/communication marks. Each study is awarded the full 3 AO1 marks, with 1 mark for the study itself and then 2 more for describing it. The essay makes six comparison points which earn the full 6 AO2 marks. The choice of studies was useful for the comparison part of the essay, as there are sufficient differences for comparisons to be made. Other points that could have been made are that both studies give a correlation only, and both studies rely at least in part on real-life data.

Treating crime

(1) Outline what is meant by zero tolerance. *(3 marks, AO1)*

(2) Outline *one* example of how the police have used zero tolerance in the reduction of crime. *(3 marks, AO1)*

(3) Evaluate zero tolerance in terms of its effectiveness. *(6 marks, AO2)*

(4) Psychology has contributed to our understanding of how aggression can be controlled. Discuss this statement. *(16 marks, essay)*

(5) Describe *two* means of controlling aggression (based on psychological findings). *(8 marks, AO1)*

(6) Evaluate *two* means of controlling aggression (based on psychological findings). *(6 marks, AO2)*

(1) You need to explain what zero tolerance means and give enough information to earn 3 marks. You could say what zero tolerance is, give a brief example and mention how it arose.

(2) Here you need to describe one example — the most straightforward one to choose is New York, 1992. You should prepare more than one example when revising, as you could be asked for two. Make sure you include enough for 3 marks.

(3) Here the focus is still on zero tolerance and you can continue with your thoughts from questions 1 and 2 above. Think of what zero tolerance is and the example you gave. You must say how effective it is — how far does it work and how far could it be said not to work? You could give other factors that could have led to a decrease in criminal behaviour (if there was a decrease, as in New York). Remember to focus on criminal behaviour, as that is what this application is about. If you are discussing the Edinburgh example, you need to think about whether the education programme and media campaign were effective in reducing male violence against women.

(4) This is an essay question. 2 marks are for clarity and communication, gained by correct use of terms, good spelling and avoiding note form. 2 marks are for balance and breadth, gained by giving a good balance of AO1 (knowledge and understanding) and AO2 (evaluation and comment), as well as presenting a clear argument. This leaves 6 AO1 marks and 6 AO2 marks. There are many ways of getting these marks. You should touch upon at least two ways of controlling aggression — make sure you use psychological terminology and preferably evidence from studies, although the latter is not essential. You could mention more than two ways. The fewer ways mentioned, the more depth you need to give. The specification only asks you to know two ways, but if you know more you could use them here. The 6 AO2 marks are for any criticisms or strengths mentioned. You could consider methods used to get evidence or how the ways seem to succeed but have limitations. You could consider ethical issues or how some ways are more effective with certain people than with others.

(5) 8 marks are available for describing two ways of controlling aggression, so assume 4 marks for each way. 2 marks are probably for knowing and giving the two methods, which leaves 3 marks each for describing them. Give enough depth for this number of marks.

(6) You do not have to evaluate the two ways you gave in question 5 above, but that would be sensible. In any case, the specification only asks you to know two ways, so you might be limited by that. Assume that there are 3 marks for each of the two ways and give criticisms. You could look at how they work, where they do not work, and if they only work for certain people. You could consider ethical issues and/or issues of social control. You could consider the theory/studies on which the means of controlling aggression are based as, if these are criticised, you might want to evaluate the ways of controlling aggression too.

■ ■ ■

Answers

(1) Zero tolerance refers to a policy used to prevent criminal acts. The main idea is that no crime should be tolerated, and any crime, however small, should be noted and the person punished appropriately. ✓ Wilson and Kelling wrote about 'broken windows' and pointed out that even one broken window in an area, if left unrepaired, could lead those in the area to think that there is no need to take care of the environment. This can lead to more broken windows and other problems such as graffiti. ✓ Quite quickly, the area can deteriorate and this suggests that from one relatively small factor a larger problem can grow. With crime, the same thing can happen. A few small incidents on the street, if unpunished, can lead to larger incidents quite quickly. Zero tolerance suggests that every small incident is punished and nothing is overlooked. ✓

e There is easily enough here for 3 marks. The answer gives the basic idea of punishing minor crimes to prevent larger ones. Then the example of 'broken windows' is given and the link to a zero tolerance policy is made clearly. Note that just a mention of 'broken windows' would not get the mark, as the point must be made clearly. The example of street crime is useful too and gets the third mark.

(2) In New York in 1992, a policy of zero tolerance was introduced. ✓ The focus was on street crime. Public drinking and the drawing of graffiti were particularly targeted. ✓ More than 7000 police officers were recruited to put the policy into effect. As would be expected, the policy led to a large increase in arrests. ✓

e The full 3 marks are given here for this example. The example itself earns 1 mark and then 2 further marks are given for elaborating and giving detail.

(3) Zero tolerance has been found to be effective as even if there are more arrests, as there were in New York, there are fewer major crimes. For example, in New York, homicides fell considerably over the period. ✓ This could, of course, have been as much a result of the 7000 extra police officers as of the actual policy. ✓ In Britain,

Pollard (1998) has been critical of zero tolerance as a policy and suggests it does not work. It is pointed out that during the New York policy, other cities in America did not adopt a zero tolerance policy and yet crime rates still fell, so it could be that something else was causing the falling crime rates in New York too. ✓✓ Bowling (1999) suggests that the drug market in the area within New York declined at the same time as the policy was introduced, so that could have accounted for the drop in major crimes, rather than the zero tolerance policy. ✓

> *e* This answer scores 5 of the 6 available marks. It focuses well on the question and gives a variety of relevant pieces of information, centred on the New York example. Another mark could have been earned for saying that when zero tolerance is introduced, it is very hard to evaluate the policy directly as there are other factors that happen at the same time. In practice, a zero tolerance policy does not tend to happen in isolation, as shown by the New York example. The whole idea of zero tolerance towards a particular crime, like domestic violence, is that all agencies will have the same zero tolerance focus, and there are likely to be media campaigns and other initiatives as well as a police 'crackdown'.

(4) Aggression is considered to be a main cause of problems in society and a large part of criminal behaviour. The control of aggression is considered to be of great importance to society, both to prevent crime and to control behaviour in institutions such as prisons. Psychologists have focused on this area and have suggested various means of controlling aggression, based on different theories. Some means of control are intended to help to prevent aggression, such as anger control programmes, and others are intended to help to control behaviour in institutions, such as token economy programmes. ✓(AO2)

Cognitive–behavioural techniques like anger control programmes are aimed at those who can learn to access their thoughts and to control those that lead to anger and aggression. ✓(AO2) Other such techniques include self-instructional training and role playing. ✓(AO1) Social skills training can form part of such programmes by helping interactions with others. This can reduce frustration and anger that might lead to aggressive behaviour. ✓(AO1) Token economy programmes use principles of operant conditioning. The idea is that appropriate (in this case, non-aggressive) behaviour should be rewarded, ✓(AO1) and inappropriate (aggressive) behaviour should either be punished or there should be negative reinforcement. ✓(AO1) Tokens can be given for appropriate behaviour after those giving the therapy have set out what this is; these are positive reinforcers. ✓(AO1) These tokens can then be exchanged for something desired, such as more television watching, a visit, or time doing exercise. ✓(AO1) These programmes do have problems. The token economy programme may work in the institution itself, although it may be difficult as there are other ways in which those in institutions are rewarded, such as by other prisoners, and these may indeed reward aggression. ✓(AO2) A problem is that even if it does work in the institution, once the individuals have left, the pattern of reinforcements will stop, and people are likely to go back to their original situation, where aggression may have been rewarded within a peer group, for example. ✓(AO2) Anger control programmes may have similar problems in that what has been learnt may not be transferred out of the setting of the programme. ✓(AO2) In addition, individuals must be able to focus on their thoughts and this suggests that aggression comes from thoughts. If it arises from biological causes, cognitive–behavioural therapy is unlikely to be helpful. ✓(AO2)

𝑒 This essay scores full marks. The answer covers more than one means of controlling aggression and focuses well on the question. It is balanced and clear, and so is awarded full balance/breadth and clarity/communication marks. 6 AO1 and 6 AO2 marks are awarded. It is difficult to separate what is description of means of controlling aggression from what is comment, but in broad terms the pure description of the method, as well as any description of underlying theory, scores AO1 marks and any comment and evaluation earns AO2 marks.

(5) Means of controlling aggression include token economy programmes used in prisons. ✓ These programmes involve principles of operant conditioning and use tokens to reward individuals for non-aggressive behaviour. ✓ Anger control programmes are also used to control aggression. ✓ These programmes use a cognitive–behavioural approach and focus on thoughts that might lead to aggressive behaviour. ✓ The individual learns to identify such thoughts and then various techniques, including social skills training, are used to help the person to react less aggressively to these thoughts. ✓

𝑒 This answer scores 5 out of 8 marks. It earns 3 marks for the outline of anger control programmes but just 2 marks for describing token economy programmes. In each case, 1 mark is for naming the programme itself. 1 mark is given for describing token economy programmes by saying that they are based on operant conditioning principles and that tokens reward behaviour. This information is very close to getting another mark but a little more needs to be said to show that 'principles of operant conditioning' are understood. A further mark could have been achieved by mentioning that tokens can then be exchanged for something desirable such as television watching. 3 marks are given for the information on anger control programmes. A further mark could have been earned by saying more about what is actually done (apart from social skills training). A mark is given for the focus on thought processes, achieved by mentioning cognitive–behavioural therapies.

(6) Self-instructional training is a way of controlling aggression and is based on cognitive–behavioural principles. A problem is that people must learn to control their thinking, and only certain sorts of people will be able to do that — they need to be able to access and understand their thoughts, and this takes a certain amount of motivation and concentration. ✓ This might not suit everyone who exhibits aggressive behaviour. Another problem with self-instructional training also applies to other techniques for controlling aggression, which is that anyone on a special programme of any kind is likely to show an improvement due to the Hawthorne effect. ✓ According to this, just being on a special programme is likely to change behaviour. Being singled out for a programme, or being given attention as a result, could be enough to lead people to change their ways, and this might include reducing aggressive behaviour. ✓ It is very hard to evaluate such programmes because of this. Another problem is that if aggression is caused by biological factors, then cognitive–behavioural programmes will not be successful. They assume that aggression comes in some way from certain thought processes and that these can be changed.

e 3 marks are given for the evaluation of self-instructional training but another means of controlling aggression is not directly addressed, so a maximum of 3 out of 6 marks are achieved. Cognitive–behavioural therapies are dealt with in general but this is unfortunately not specific enough. The answer could have involved another cognitive–behavioural therapy, such as anger control programmes, and then the general criticisms could have been applied to both, thus gaining the other 3 marks.